STANDARD LOAN

Renew Books on PHONE-it: 01443 654456

Books are to be returned on or before the last date below

Glyntaff Learning Resources Centre
University of Glamorgan CF37 4BD

SPORTING SKILLS SERIES

Wicketkeeping

BOB TAYLOR

WITH THE ASSISTANCE OF PATRICK MURPHY

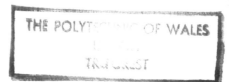
PELHAM BOOKS

First published in Great Britain by
PELHAM BOOKS LTD
52 Bedford Square
London WC1B 3EF
1979

*Thanks are due to the following for permission to reproduce photographs: to
Patrick Eagar for those on pages 14–15, 22–3, 27, 44–5, 46–7, 48–9, 51, 56,
58, 60, 61, 66–7, 68–9, 70–1, 72, 77, 78, 100, 101, 102, 108, 109, 114, 116,
120; to Ken Kelly for those on pages 13, 53, 59, 74, 75, 82, 98, 103, 105,
106, 111, 112, 115, 118; to the* Press Association Ltd *for those on pages 94,
95, 96, 97; to the* Northampton Chronicle and Echo *for that on page 18;
and to the* Northampton Evening Telegraph *for that on page 29.*

ISBN 0 7207 1142 8

Phototypeset in Great Britain by
Western Printing Services Ltd, Bristol

Printed by Hollen Street Press, at Slough, Berkshire
and bound by Dorstel Press at Harlow, Essex

Contents

Foreword by Bob Willis

I'm delighted Bob Taylor's at last put his thoughts on his art in book form, not least because he's such a master of the craft of keeping wicket. But there's more to Bob than just consistent brilliance behind the stumps; his approachable attitude towards inquisitive youngsters, keen club cricketers and fellow professionals is equally consistent. Nothing's too much trouble for Bob Taylor – he tells everyone how lucky he's been, and that it's only right that he should pass on the kind of advice he received when learning his trade.

In the England team he's known as 'Chat', because he's so enviably polite and attentive at the endless cocktail parties and social functions that a tour party must always attend. And if ever I had to pick my all-time World Eleven, the twelfth man would be Bob Taylor, not because he isn't good enough (far from it) but in tribute to his unrivalled qualities as a team-mate. I've been on five England tours with Bob – the first when I was a skinny youngster under Ray Illingworth. When I flew out to replace the injured Alan Ward, it was Bob who met me at the airport, nursed me along and gave me the sort of kind encouragement only he can offer. He's been an object lesson to us all in simple unselfishness and dedicated professionalism. And what a keeper! In this book he mentions the stumping of Chadwick off Geoff Boycott's bowling and the catch off my bowling to dismiss Brendon Bracewell. Both were fantastic efforts, typical of his unobtrusive art.

How Bob maintained the quality of his keeping in a mediocre county side and as number two to Alan Knott for so many years was astonishing. I never heard him moan or say a cheap thing about Knotty – and I can think of many in the game who would have reacted differently. Now Bob's had his reward for all those years of patience and dedication. He's unashamedly proud to be England's wicketkeeper, and as his team-mate and close friend I'm proud to have been part of his career. I wish Bob and Pat Murphy every success with a book that'll teach cricketers of all ages so much.

1 What Makes a Wicketkeeper?

If I hadn't got fed up with fielding on the boundary at the tender age of nine, I would never have kept wicket for England. The ball just never seemed to come near me. I wanted to be in the game – as centre forward for my school team it was great to see the name 'Taylor' underlined in red ink on the noticeboard every time I scored. It was the same with cricket . . . I fancied seeing 'stumped Taylor' and 'caught Taylor' in the scorebook, so I badgered my sportsmaster to give me a go behind the stumps. My passion for keeping had begun – and it's never ended.

So to the schoolboy and the club player who wants to keep wicket, my first question is: do you want to be in the thick of the action? The wicketkeeper should be the inspiration to the rest of the side in the field. You want the fielder to think, 'Wasn't that a great catch?' or, 'Didn't he take that bad return well?' Many players in club cricket take the keeper for granted, but he's the most decisive player on the field, even more than the skipper. The keeper mustn't be self-conscious; people say to me that I swashbuckle around the field, but I hope it doesn't look that way. I'm just enjoying myself and trying to communicate an aura of confidence and buoyancy to the rest of the fielders. In my time Godfrey Evans and Alan Knott have been marvellous at geeing up the side near the end of the day's play when it's hot and everyone's flagging, although other great keepers have done this in a quieter way.

Whatever the methods, the keeper's the conductor, the orchestrator, of a good fielding performance. If he's good at his craft – if he takes his catches, stumps the batsmen, saves overthrows and tidies up the fielding – then automatically the side's a better one.

This is particularly important in limited-over cricket, whether it's at county level or even the 20-over biff and bash of night-time club cricket.

Because the keeper's so involved tactically in the game he must love his cricket. When I was a nipper I'd played in the street with the rest of the boys, for my school and even on the cinder car park at Stoke City's football ground, but I was thirteen when I was really hooked. My sportsmaster took me to his local club, fifteen miles away at Bignall End. It was my first trip in a motorcar (that was exciting enough) but I'll never forget the atmosphere of club cricket that night. Aaron Lockett, who was to be my coach, was in his sixties at the time, still playing and sewing the pads and gloves to save money, the pavilion was immaculate, and I still can smell the linseed oil on the bats. For me it was out of this world, especially as the club thought I had ability as a keeper.

But I was so green. I was thirteen when I played my first match for the Under Eighteens in the very strong Kidsgrove League. I had no proper gear, I wore a white shirt, black plimsolls, grey flannels and I was so small the pads were halfway up my chest. As I staggered out to keep wicket the groundsman shouted, 'Have you got a box on, lad?' In my innocence I stuttered, 'What's a box?' and couldn't understand why the groundsman laughed his head off. Well, I asked questions, found out the purpose of an abdominal protector, pestered my mum and finally got one for a few bob.

I wanted to make the thirty-mile round trip every night. I practised for hours, coached by the former England player Jack Ikin and by Aaron Lockett, a fine all-rounder, and I never thought I could be so happy. School would end at 4 pm, I'd have tea at my sportsmaster's house, and then he'd drive me to Bignall End. Then when I left school I'd go there five nights a week and never bat an eyelid at sitting in a bus for two hours. Life and its aims were simple – I wanted to keep wicket all summer round, and the idea of eventually getting paid to do just that was like a dream.

So now when I coach young wicketkeepers, I want to see if they love the game. Things are easier for them now: their parents can afford to buy them the proper gear and the motorcar means they can get more easily to matches. All this has made youngsters today less conscientious about learning the sport – I'm not just being nostalgic, I really believe it's true that many of them take too much for granted. So I want to see genuine enthusiasm from the young keeper. He must look as if he's enjoying himself. There's no need to show off – many of those who indulge in showmanship in club or schoolboy cricket are the ones who drop the ball regularly. He must be on his toes and agile. I'm looking for someone whose fingers point downwards when he takes the ball, someone with a natural pair of hands that 'give' whenever he takes the ball. He must let it come to him, rather than snatch at it. He'll be calm with a rhythmic motion that'll take the ball and rock back towards the stumps in one easy, fluid motion. I don't want to see him break the stumps every time the ball passes the bat – he must be cool enough to try for a stumping only when it's possible, not just to impress his team-mates, because they'll soon get fed up with the game stopping and starting for this.

I try to assess natural ability, then build on it. So at the beginner's stage, agility is more important than fitness. I'm talking about one-day cricketers, not seven-day-a-week professionals, although you'd be amazed how many county keepers don't move their feet enough and can't get their bodies behind the ball at crucial moments. The promising young keeper should be on his toes all the time, anticipating the ball. Of course he's got to be fit – with all that sprinting, crouching, trotting and diving, he'll eventually have to be the fittest in his side – but for the moment, lightness of movement's more necessary.

He should be a good fielder anywhere. Some of you playing school or club cricket who read this may not be keepers, but if you can field well, you've got the basics – anticipation, agility, good catching hands, the ability to sprint, and judgement. Provided you're not too tall or fat, you should think about being a wicket-keeper if fed up with fielding, and that applies even if you're the wrong side of thirty.

It also helps if you've got ball sense, if you're good at other sports. Most of the professionals I know can play football, golf or tennis, and the best game for a keeper is squash. Those sudden changes of direction quicken your reactions, it's great for stamina and all that low bending's invaluable training. And after chasing a small, dark ball in artificial light, a red cricket ball in daylight looks very large indeed.

One vital thing – you must never think of getting hurt. It's like the footballer who worries about breaking his leg: if he goes into a tackle half-heartedly, he's got every chance of a bad knock. I was playing with a hard ball at eight and thoughts of injury just didn't enter my head. Keep your head over the ball – in nearly twenty years of first-class cricket I've had just one chipped finger from keeping wicket. I agree that school and club wickets are often dodgy, but if you're enjoying keeping wicket, getting hurt will be the last thing on your mind.

Have pride in your standards, whoever you're representing. I think it's a sin to drop a straightforward catch standing back. I'll never forget spilling Alan Jones once when Derbyshire played Glamorgan. Alan Ward was bowling, it was a simple nick, I saw it all the way, and it went straight in and out. Alan just stood there open-mouthed; I'm not being big-headed but I have my standards and I was disgusted with myself, even though Alan was amused afterwards.

One over from the Derbyshire inswing bowler Ian Buxton stopped me taking anything for granted ever again. It was a John Player match against Glamorgan and I dropped Roy Fredericks three times! Two of the snicks were attempted drives and they just went in and out, and the third was even easier – Roy played forward, and got a tickle. I wanted to hide and I realized why; the day before I'd played at Lord's for MCC against the Champion County and I thought I'd really made it. That's the only time I've been guilty of over-confidence, and whenever anybody kindly praises my ability to maintain a certain standard, I feel grateful to Roy Fredericks.

There's a world of difference between over-confidence (which saps your concentration) and pride in your work. I've always believed in my ability, and only once in first-class cricket have I had my doubts. That was in 1964, when I hurt my ankle playing football for Port Vale. The Derbyshire captain, Charlie Lee, played an extra batsman, Laurie Johnson, for the first eight matches of that season and it looked as if I wouldn't get back. I was worried, but some kind souls in the press box gave the club a hammering and I was in again – and my soccer days were numbered.

So believe in yourself, otherwise the team won't benefit from your skills. Gee them up, take on tactical responsibility – you're in a unique position behind the stumps to help your captain. But take all the praise in your stride. I admire the quiet, confident ones. It suits my personality, and I like to see someone gracious when he's done well while aware at the same time that next day you can be on your ear with a great bump.

Be self-critical. When I'm keeping badly, I know it's because of three things: I've lost my concentration, I'm getting up too quickly from my usual crouched position, or I'm snatching at the ball. The art of mental discipline's so important to a keeper at every level. I'm not saying you should walk around on the field with a face like a wet weekend, but you must train yourself to expect the ball to come to you every time. If I had my way, every dressing room in the country would have a notice on the wall for the keeper – 'THE NEXT BALL'S COMING TO YOU.' Any stumper at any level is a better one if he trains his mind and concentrates harder.

A loss of concentration can be disastrous at first-class level. In the Benson and Hedges final against Kent, we desperately needed Bob Woolmer back in the pavilion. We'd made a low score and Woolmer was the sheet anchor for Kent. Eddie Barlow dropped him at first slip off Mike Hendrick, and for a few moments we were all naturally despondent. Well I didn't clear my mind quickly enough, I wasn't really ready for the next ball – so I dropped Woolmer when a great delivery from Hendrick nicked the shoulder of his bat. I saw it, hesitated for that thousandth of a second,

didn't get fully across to it, and the ball touched the ends of my fingers and popped out. Woolmer won the 'Man of the Match' award and Kent won comfortably. Normally I would have caught that nick, but I wasn't concentrating fully on the next ball.

One thing that'll sap your concentration and make you a lesser keeper is poor, ill-fitting equipment. If you're bothered by something as trivial as a tight cap, or pads that are tight, or boots that are pinching, you won't be at your best. Make yourself fussy, take no notice of the lads in the clubhouse who pull your leg. Wear a shirt that's a size too big so you won't feel tight under the arms. Always wear a vest – you mustn't get a chill on the field, because a warm keeper will be that much more agile and alert. Never wear a long-sleeved sweater – they're just too bulky for a keeper. If it's cold and windy or damp, wear two sleeveless sweaters.

Eddie Barlow and myself trying hard to carry out the maxim that's vital for all wicketkeepers and close fielders: 'Every ball's coming to you'

13

You need to be naturally athletic to keep wicket — but you also need to be confident about your equipment. In this instance I could go for the spectacular legside dive to take a loose one from Ian Botham because I was one-hundred-per-cent happy about my loose-fitting shirt and all the other gear. I could concentrate on the job in hand without worrying about an ill-fitting pair of pads or gloves

If you've got any pride in your ability, you must have your own gloves. Get hold of a pair somehow and take them home with you after a match. And another thing – never wet your inner gloves. Over the years I've seen many keepers do this because they've been lazy and left them screwed up in a ball from the previous match. But if you smooth them out they'll be supple for the next time and you won't risk arthritic hands from wearing wet inners season after season. Of course the inners have to be moist, otherwise your gloves just won't feel right, so for about five minutes before you take the field, put on your inners and gloves and get a couple of fast bowlers to bowl at you. The sweat you will work up will moisten your inners.

I hear a lot of keepers talk about taping their fingers before taking the field. I think this theory dates from the days when the gloves weren't all that thick and the tapes were needed to support the joints. Apart from my early county days when I used tape to support the weak joints, I've never bothered – it gets a drag pulling all the sticky parts off, and quite honestly, the quality gloves today are sufficient protection if you're taking the ball properly.

If you're standing all day behind the stumps, your feet must feel comfortable. That's why I wear soft tennis shoes, although on a damp day I'll wear spikes to avoid slipping. Test the surface before you field. It's no use complaining about the surface after you've dropped a catch. I remember getting a shock at Adelaide once when playing for the Rest of the World against Australia. It was fine and dry, and just before lunch the spinners Bishen Bedi and Intikhab Alam were brought on. I came up to the wicket, only to find myself slipping around like a novice skater. The groundsman had scattered grass cuttings just behind the stumps and I could hardly stand, let alone keep to a couple of world-class spinners! I made straight for my spikes during the lunch interval, I can tell you . . .

Right, let's assume our keen would-be stumper has all the right equipment. What else is needed? A good pair of eyes and ears for a start. Eyes to watch better keepers and ears to listen to advice.

Take notice of the coaching books, but don't treat them as a bible. Although I respect coaches, you have to do what's natural. If you're feeling natural behind the stumps, you're relaxed and calm and on the way to being good at the job. But listen to what others say; I've seen men who've played for England fall by the wayside because they thought they knew it all.

I was unbelievably lucky with my advisers at Bignall End. Neither Jack Ikin nor Aaron Lockett had ever been keepers, but they taught me so much about concentration and making the best of your talents. Imagine having a former England player playing for the same club side! How many youngsters have that luck? Now I try to do for the young lads what Jack and Aaron did for me. Cricket's such an education that the beginner needs all the help he can get. And not just the beginner – when I got back into the England team I had the great pleasure of a chat with the old Warwickshire and England keeper, 'Tiger' Smith. He was over ninety at the time, but still very shrewd, and spoke with great knowledge and authority on the art of wicketkeeping. If ever I needed proof that you're never too old to learn, it was that chat with dear old 'Tiger'.

Have your heroes, too. Go and watch them at Tests or in county games, and try to learn things from them. Pluck up courage and ask their advice. I went to Old Trafford three times as a boy, each time to watch Godfrey Evans, and then at the age of twenty-two I was again at Manchester to watch my big hero, Keith Andrew, playing only his second game for England. I can see him now against the West Indies, standing up to Ted Dexter's erratic medium pace and making the legside takes look so easy. He gave away three byes out of a total of 501 in that match, made a brave nightwatchman's 15 against Hall and Griffith, and was dropped for the next Test! So much for the keeper being a specialist.

Keith never seemed to miss a catch or a stumping. He was always behind the ball. I was still a club cricketer when I saw him play in some charity matches in Staffordshire. He was known as 'Mr Smoothie' by his Northants colleagues and he just radiated a quiet confidence. I respected him so much that I called him 'Mr

Andrew' when I played for Derbyshire early in my career against Northamptonshire. I've never seen anyone to touch Keith Andrew, and those kind folk who say there's a lot of Keith in my wicketkeeping are very flattering but wrong. Nobody could be as good as him, and I just hope I've got some of his qualities.

My idol, Keith Andrew, the greatest I've ever seen. A supreme craftsman and a model to the young hopeful Bob Taylor

In my early days Keith helped me get some super gloves. He got his from that great old keeper Bertie Oldfield, in Sydney, and as well as giving me an old pair, Keith gave me Bertie's address. I was entitled to a free pair from the club, so I wrote to Bertie and eight weeks later I had the great pleasure of donning my beautiful new gloves and giving the Derbyshire secretary a bill for £25! And since 1961, I've used only three pairs of gloves, so Keith's judgement wasn't bad . . .

But even if the ambitious wicketkeeper's got the right attitude, natural ability, fitness and intelligence, he can still come unstuck. He could go to a club that seems snobbish, with players who don't make the new arrival welcome. A shy youngster can struggle in these circumstances, but if he swallows hard, remains polite and respectful and asks questions about the game, he'll make his presence felt eventually. Try to be modest but confident at the same time; you can waste valuable years by being too shy.

Yet in the end luck plays an important part. In my case it was luck that gave me a cricket-mad sportsmaster who was also Bignall End's secretary; it was luck that Jack Ikin and Aaron Lockett were there with such a wealth of knowledge; it was luck when the former England bowler Cliff Gladwin saw me playing in the North Staffs League and recommended me to the county. I was lucky that George Dawkes dropped out through injury after many injury-free seasons as soon as I joined Derbyshire. And of course, Kerry Packer's been lucky for me. I'd almost given up all hope of getting more than one England cap, then my great friend Alan Knott takes Packer's money and the selectors are looking for an experienced specialist wicketkeeper rather than one who can score hundreds.

Of course, I've worked hard at every stage of my cricket to raise my standards, but I reckon the gods were smiling on me that day when nine-year-old Bob Taylor decided he wanted some glory behind the stumps.

2 Mental Demands

Whatever the class of cricket, you'll be a better wicketkeeper if you sort out your mental approach. Of all the fielders, the keeper just can't afford to be slapdash, and if you can train your mind so that you're expecting every ball to go straight into your gloves, then you'll be that much better at the task.

The longer I stay in the game, the more difficult I find the mental demands. Many are due to the pressures of Tests, but I really have to gear myself up to returning to play for Derbyshire immediately after the Test ends. Of course it's nothing personal, but I'm sure you can understand the difference between keeping to different bowlers in front of 20,000 at Lord's, then stepping out the next cold morning at Derby in front of a handful of loyal spectators. So as I get older I have to concentrate harder, and I'm mentally shattered at the end of the day's play.

Of course you can't concentrate every second of the game when you're out in the field, so you have to train yourself to switch off at certain moments. Once the bowler's got the ball and he's walking back to his mark I'll have a look around, exchange a quick word with the slips and then as the bowler starts to run in again I'm telling myself, 'This one's coming to me.'

It's more difficult to switch off with a slow bowler because there's little time to let your mind wander. But while he's walking back I look at a spot where I think the ball's going to land, and then just as he's about to bowl I'll re-focus on the bowler. This helps keep my head down, and if the bowler's a medium-pacer and I'm standing up to him, I'll have time to do it twice between deliveries. Nobody taught me to do this, I thought it out myself, but as a matter of interest I have noticed that the great golfer Jack

Nicklaus looks at a particular spot just ahead of him before he looks up to drive off the tee, and I wonder if that's equally beneficial to him.

You mustn't get too distracted by the slips – you haven't really got time for more than a few words. Don't worry if some of them think you're too serious because you don't talk much between deliveries – there's plenty of time for the cheerful banter between the overs. Mike Brearley's the best concentrater I've had beside me at slip, while Graham Roope's been the worst. Poor Graham just never shuts up, even when the bowler's running in. I've often had to tell him to belt up during a Test, and I'm sure he'd be an even finer slip than he already is if he concentrated more. Obviously nervous energy's got a lot to do with his chattering, and I've seen him take some absolute blinders at slip, but he seems to waste some of his marvellous natural ability by lack of concentration.

If you're mentally tough you can triumph over a lack of natural ability at any 'level. You can be like Geoff Boycott, who's so dedicated and determined that he made himself into a top-class batsman. He really psychs himself up before going out to bat and during the various intervals, and in my own way I work at my mental process as well.

For a couple of minutes before the bell goes to take the field I'll sit on my own and think about the batsmen we're going to face. I'll analyse their strengths and, more important, their weaknesses. In the past, good players like John Whitehouse, Harry Pilling or Brian Luckhurst have all had a tendency to glance fine down the legside and I've prepared myself for such a chance. Most of the fine overseas batsmen give you hope outside the off stump early in their innings, so I'll make a mental note of that. With a left-hander like John Edrich, who likes to leg glance very fine, I've got to be ready to go a long way if he's facing a right-arm bowler over the wicket. I'll be standing back wider on the off so I can see the bowler's delivery – therefore if the left-hander snicks fine that means about an extra five yards I'll have to cover to my right side to get near the ball.

Alan Knott has had to travel a long way to get this legside catch, because he'll have been standing outside off stump for the left-hander. The unlucky batsman is Australia's Rodney Marsh

I'm always geared up at the start of play, always expecting a catch off the first ball. There's no reason why you club keepers shouldn't be the same – if you play regularly for your side, you'll recognize the opposition's best batsmen season after season, and know what to expect of them if your memory's good enough. And there's often a left-hand opener in the opposition team, so get ready for that legside glance.

There are times though when all your planning, all your professionalism works – but the umpire ruins the golden moment. Picture the scene . . . Derbyshire against Hampshire at Chesterfield with Barry Richards, then the best opener in the world, walking out to take strike. We tried him first ball in his vulnerable off-stump area, he snicked Alan Ward, I caught him one-handed diving in front of first slip. Barry wouldn't go, the umpire Ron Aspinall said: 'Not out', and we couldn't believe it. Half an hour after lunch he was out for 153.

Such things happen much more in club cricket, and it's really frustrating. The umpire could be just wiping the sleep out of his eyes, dozing off after a lunchtime pint or bearing a grudge against his own club's bowler or keeper. I know it's difficult, but when the decision goes against you and the batsman stays put, don't lose your temper. Think to yourself, 'Right, you ——, we'll get you out a second time now.' If you get sidetracked into slanging matches, you're not keeping wicket well.

So much for planning the pre-lunch session in the keeper's mind. What about lunchtime? Well, when I come off the field I'll immediately take off my gloves and pads and place them beside me, ready to pick up again without any hurry or fluster. Then off come my shoes and socks, I'll put some sandals on, rest my feet and just wind down for a few blissful minutes. The twelfth man will bring me a cup of hot sweet tea, a cheese roll and an icecream. I'd like to think the club or school keeper would be treated in the same way by his team-mates. If they realize he's not being a prima donna but an important member of the side who shouldn't have to queue for his cuppa, then one of his fellow fielders – say, a batsman – should bring his lunch or tea to him.

When the first bell sounds, fifteen minutes before the post-lunch session begins, I'll start thinking again about the day's play. By the second bell – five minutes to go – I'll have a clean pair of socks on, then the rest of my equipment, and I'll have a quick word with the bowlers about the not-out batsmen.

At close of play, I'll have a pint of beer straight away and take about thirty minutes to unwind. I'll sit wiggling my toes, chat about the day's play and then have a long soak in the bath. I don't stop thinking about the cricket till I've left the ground, and then I like to forget all about it till the following morning. If you don't train yourself to switch off from cricket at some stage, you'll be mentally unfit for the following day – it can be a bore to get asked about the happenings on the field that day at social functions. Believe it or not, I like to hear about other people's jobs, not mine, when I'm away from the cricket.

But I must stress that between the hours of play the keeper must concentrate on concentration all the time. I still get reminders of this when I keep badly. In a Test in New Zealand, Geoff Boycott was skipper, and when play resumed after the weekend break I soon had an attack of the 'Monday morning blues' – that feeling all professional cricketers dread. I felt listless, just couldn't concentrate, and when Bob Willis bowled one that deviated after it passed the stumps, I only got my fingers to the ball, it went for one bye and looked very sloppy. Both Willis and Boycott gave me a well-deserved rocket, but the rest of the side then proceeded to field sloppily. I was to blame, because a good side takes its fielding standard from the wicketkeeper, and England that morning were let down by me.

And don't relax in the last over, either. Don't start thinking about that cool pint of bitter, that long, lazy bath, as the bowler's on his way to the stumps. One of my most satisfying stumpings was off Derek Underwood against South Australia at Adelaide, when I was playing for the England touring team on Ray Illingworth's tour. Barry Richards had batted all day for 146, it was hot, the wicket was flat and hard. In the last over, Richards danced down the wicket and missed. It wasn't a difficult stumping, but I could so easily have fumbled it, and I was pleased my vigilance hadn't slackened at the end of a hot day.

The observant keeper will also watch out for lapses of concentration in other fielders – and it happens at Test level, I assure you. Phil Edmunds, a very talented spin bowler, is an example. His mind wanders sometimes, he tries too many variations in the same over, loses concentration when bowling bad balls and gets annoyed at himself and the fielders. He bowled New Zealand's Bev Congdon with an absolute beauty at the Oval, but not before Mike Brearley and myself had had to gee him up. Just before, Phil bowled two superb deliveries at Congdon that just missed, and I noticed Phil's head start to drop. I said to Mike Brearley, 'He's off day-dreaming again,' Mike said something deliberately provocative to him, and the next ball pitched just outside the leg stump, turned in the rough and hit the top of the off stump. Poor Bev said, 'You can't play those can you?' and I couldn't help agreeing. Full marks to Brearley, though, for getting Phil's mind back on the job.

I'm often asked, 'Are you nervous playing in front of a large Test crowd?' I love it when I'm out there, but all players get nervous just before taking the field in a Test match. Even unflappable characters like Tony Greig shake a bit when they're puffing at a final fag, I've seen Mike Brearley's hands shaking badly before going out to bat, and Derek Randall was always in and out of the toilet just before the start. The secret is to leave your tension behind in the dressing room. I learned a lot about mental strength from Eddie Barlow when he captained Derbyshire for two and a half marvellous seasons. He had a great, unworried philosophy about the game, and the fact that he was thirty-six before he ever played in the daily grind of English professional cricket, and then had to carry the cares of captaincy too, showed how mentally tough he was. Yet Eddie worried about the game off the field – in his first full season as captain, he had a nervous rash on one of his hands. He'd often be up till the early hours of the morning, sorting the team out in his mind, but his greatness was that the players didn't know any of this.

26

The wicketkeeper with the greatest mental discipline in my time has undoubtedly been Alan Knott. To maintain his high standards through so many Test series was fantastic; he was almost like Geoff Boycott in his rigid self-discipline. He wouldn't stay long at the social functions on tour, he'd personally supervise the laundering of his cricket gear back at the hotel, rather than hang it on the dressing room line like the other players, and he was obsessive about his food. During his Test career he met a Californian who was over ninety at the time, looked about fifty, and had loads of grandchildren. He influenced Knotty's eating habits greatly – even down to having honey in his tea. Towards the end of his Test career Knotty suffered criticism for occasionally slipping from his own incredibly high standards, but he was easily the most dedicated keeper I've known.

A graphic example of the kind of concentration needed to keep wicket at Test level. You can see on Alan Knott's face how vital it is to get that ball back from the field, because he thinks he's got a great chance of running out Rodney Marsh. In fact, Marsh is easily home, but in his vigilance Knott hasn't really noticed

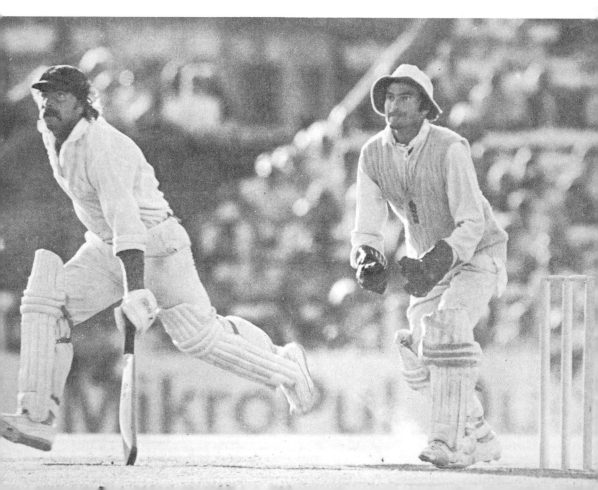

Australia's Rod Marsh was another who toughened up his mental approach. He had a bad first series against Ray Illingworth's touring side – critics christened him 'Ironfists', and I spoke to him in the dressing room sometimes when he was very depressed. But a year later I returned to Australia with the Rest of the World side to find a slimmed-down Marsh. He was still muscular, but now much quicker on his feet, and against Mike Denness's England team he was leaping around like a salmon, taking spectacular catches off Lillee and Thomson. The influence of his golfing brother, Graham, was decisive I think. On Denness's tour I had dinner with the two Marsh brothers and their father. Graham said he was set to earn so many thousand dollars playing golf for a Japanese TV station for just two days on a Pacific Island. Rod's jaw dropped open; he said, 'That's as much as I've earned in the last four years of cricket,' and then he buckled down to his task. He saw what he had to do if he wanted to be a successful sportsman and I admired him for his determination. And incidentally that dinner-time revelation by Graham Marsh probably had a lot to do with Rod's decision to throw over official Test cricket and take Kerry Packer's money.

I've seen many English keepers in county cricket with stacks of talent but with that crucial lack of iron will and concentration. Laurie Johnson of Northants was a classic case – he succeeded Keith Andrew behind the stumps and had many of his skills. He'd look superb one day – smooth legside takes, effortless stumpings in the Andrew mould – but then he'd keep like a novice, missing easy stumpings, letting byes through the gloves or taking a throw sloppily. A man with tremendous natural ability, he just lacked that necessary mental discipline.

Geoff Clayton, a really fine batsman/keeper, was another. In his career at Lancashire and Somerset he was nicknamed 'Chimp' because of his walk and long arms – he was a coalman in the winter – but instead of just accepting the nickname, Geoff would fool around and play for laughs. He didn't seem to realize that underneath the banter from his colleagues was a deep respect for his skills. So Geoff never really did himself justice.

Laurie Johnson, the Northants keeper of a few years back — all the natural skills, but he lacked that crucial mental strength

Jimmy Binks of Yorkshire was a very different kettle of fish. He played so many consecutive county matches that he must have been very resilient mentally and physically to overcome the knocks that you'll always pick up. And he stood up to many bowlers – not just spinners like Illingworth, Wardle and Don Wilson but seamers like Tony Nicholson and Bob Appleyard. I've seen Jimmy take some great legside stumpings off Nicholson's quicker 'dart' ball. A great concentrator was Jimmy Binks.

The man who's succeeded Jimmy as Yorkshire's regular keeper still lacks his mental strength. David Bairstow's attitude and ability are first-class, but he's taken rather longer to push his way into an England touring party than I would have thought. I've talked to David many times about his lapses in concentration, and he really wants to listen and learn, but little avoidable errors mar his performance. I don't think some of the Yorkshire players or members help him much, though. I remember a bad performance by David against Derbyshire in a John Player match at Huddersfield. He had dropped John Edrich off a simple chance the day before in a Benson and Hedges Cup match at a crucial stage, and when I talked to him before our game I could see it was still bothering David. He agreed he was snatching at the ball, that he wasn't moving his feet quickly enough or concentrating properly, but he still kept badly. He missed stumping one of our lads when he was three yards out of his crease, and to make matters worse I got a stumping off Geoff Miller. Afterwards David was even more depressed when a member said, 'That's the way to stump a batsman, David.' Such so-called encouragement is no help to a basically fine keeper who just needs to concentrate harder.

David and Lancashire's John Lyon are the only two county keepers who've ever asked me to watch them at the start of a Derbyshire innings and then comment afterwards on their displays. Yet John, even more than David Bairstow, lacks self-confidence and mental toughness. Some of the Lancashire players give him a hard time, and he often looks as if he shouldn't be out there in the middle. Yet I rate him highly; he just needs regular confidence boosting. I've often said, 'Well kept, John,' at the close of play and he'll reply tentatively, 'Do you think so, Bob?' A keeper must be calmly confident about his own skills.

Andy Brassington of Gloucestershire is another young keeper I rate highly, yet he used to get depressed about playing little regular first-team cricket because his county played Andy Stovold, a batsman who could also keep wicket. Andy's parents live half a mile from me, and I've had many chats with him about the importance of sticking to good habits and remembering his good technique behind the stumps – but it's difficult when you can't get regular chances to show those talents in county cricket.

This is a vintage time for young English wicketkeepers, and the one I rate most highly is Nottinghamshire's Bruce French. When he was sixteen he came over to Chesterfield to ask my advice, particularly about concentration, and whenever I've played against him he's looked very good. He seems to have Keith Andrew's calmness, and I'm delighted to see he always picks his spot on the wicket and concentrates very hard between deliveries. And playing with the Young England side has helped to instil mental toughness at an early age. Definitely one to watch.

The mental pressure is the main reason why fine young keepers like Paul Downton, Brassington, French and Lyon aren't also run-scoring batsmen. I don't think it's fair to expect a keeper to win many matches with the bat, because his role demands so much concentration that he can't be expected to walk out with the bat within a few minutes. People will say I'm biased because my batting's never been very successful, but in the past only Les Ames, Alan Knott and, to a lesser extent, South Africa's Dennis Lindsay and John Waite have managed to combine both roles. Whether we're talking about club cricket, the school grade, minor counties or first-class cricket, if the wicketkeeper's good enough, his ability to concentrate hard for long periods will be decisive – and it's unfair to expect much more from him.

3 Physical Pressures

At any level of cricket, a wicketkeeper with the right sort of attitude must be fit. He'll travel hundreds of miles between both sets of stumps every season; he'll be in the crouch position hundreds of times in a day; if a fast bowler's operating, he'll run on average twice an over to the stumps; and then if he's still got enough bounce and energy he'll trot to the other end after every over. He should be the fittest man in the side, fitter even than the fast bowler who puts everything into his over yet can relax walking back to the mark rather than have to crouch down six times in a row – and the bowler also gets a rest before his next over.

At first-class level, the limited-over brand of cricket really has helped improve physical-fitness standards. You've got to be fit to climb into a car on a Saturday night after a day's play, travel possibly a couple of hundred miles for a John Player game, run around in the field for forty overs then travel back that night to resume the championship game the next day. And the limited-over game puts extra pressure on the keeper – he's running up to the stumps more, because more risks are taken and chances of run-outs are greater, and without a slip he's got a very wide area to cover.

At no stage should the stumper think, 'God, I'm shattered,' because if he's worried about his fitness he'll lose concentration. This is where the club or schoolboy player with guts and common sense can use the same techniques as the professionals to get fit. He doesn't have to worry about poor facilities or lack of money and opportunity. If he concentrates on four things – body expercises, a running programme, regular practice and a balanced, nutritious diet – the keeper at any level can be nearly as fit as the county players.

The body exercises can be done in the front room, the bedroom or even at the ground. They're done on the day of a match and they're designed to make the body supple and resilient. There's a lot of stress on a keeper's body because he's in an unnatural position for so long – he can rick his back when running up to the wicket and twisting awkwardly for a bad return, he can tear his Achilles tendon by crouching on the balls of his feet with his heels in the air for long periods, and his legs, calves and thighs can also feel the strain.

About three quarters of an hour before the start of play, whether or not I'm due to keep wicket, I'll start my exercises. I concentrate on waist exercises so I'm flexible from the waist, but I'll start from the top and work systematically down to my toes. I begin by twisting my head from side to side for two minutes to get rid of nervous tension. Then the shoulders – with the legs apart, throw the hands across your chest for two minutes either side. Then press the arms into the chest and fling them back behind the shoulders as far as possible – again two minutes for each side.

Now it's the waist. For another two minutes, put your hands on your hips, keep the feet still and swing your shoulders from side to side. Then the vital thigh area that takes so much of the strain on the keeper's body. My speciality here is what I call my Cossack routine – get down into a crouch position and throw your feet out like a Cossack dancer. Two minutes for that one. It takes a lot of time to master but will prove invaluable to you. Then another test for the thighs – sit up against a wall and push yourself upright. The thighs take the body strain and you'll feel their strength as you get up. Start on thirty seconds for this one, and then build up to a minute.

Now one for the groin. Extend your right leg behind you with the right foot parallel to the wall, place your right hand on your right buttock, and the left leg should be taut in front of you, taking the strain. Press down on the right buttock ten times and you'll feel just a gentle tugging on the groin. Then change over and repeat the exercise for the front right foot. Sounds painful, I know, but it'll avoid the groin strains you get when pulling up sharply from the crouch position or when diving.

A simple exercise for the calves and Achilles. Sit on your backside for two minutes on the floor and just wiggle your toes backwards and forwards.

Now I know what some of you are thinking – 'I'll look soft doing all this in front of the team.' You won't. Ignore them. They'll be the ones who look soft if they miss games through injury. If they keep pulling your leg at the ground, go somewhere quiet to do the exercises. This programme takes just fifteen minutes, and whether you're over thirty and want to get into the first team at the club, or a shy, spotty kid in the school thirds, you'll be a better keeper if you go through it before a match.

Right, let's assume you're feeling supple and ready for some fielding practice before the match starts. My first move is to get the fast bowlers to send a few down into my gloves from twenty-two yards on the outfield. Mark out the distance, and ask them to bowl normal line and length for about ten minutes. This'll help you get the feel of the ball and get your inners moist, as well as helping the bowler loosen up.

Then I do a difficult one that's very useful if done properly. The keeper and three slips stand on the outfield in their normal positions behind the batsman. The bowler throws the ball on the full toss to the batsman, who leans back and edges the ball in our direction. It's a realistic exercise, because the ball won't be following the predictable line you get with a cradle or if someone's throwing the ball at you. But you need an accurate thrower and a batsman with a good enough eye to snick the ball hard at various angles. Ken Barrington's been marvellous as the batsman whenever he's been England's manager on tour – though I do remember he was hit a painful blow on the elbow by a wild thrower once in Pakistan!

Is it worth a keeper practising in the nets? Few in the county game bother going into a net, because there's rarely any room behind the stumps. With three of four bowlers in each net, it's artificial for the keeper because you get no breathing space, you're up and down far too quickly. There should be a pace to your wicketkeeping, and if practising in the nets gets you out of a calm, unhurried pace, pack it in. But if you do go in a net, start off with neither batsman nor stumps and ask one bowler to send the deliveries down on a particular spot. Tell him to take his time, so you get into the habit of watching a part of the wicket and building up your concentration. Then ask him to send down some full half-volleys; they're the most difficult to gather because they're near your feet and they skid through once they've pitched.

Then, if you can, ask a batsman to come into the net. Ask him to play at some of the full half-volleys but leave a few so that you just have to take the skidding, low ball. Now I realize you need a patient batsman and a very accurate bowler for this one – and I've been lucky with men like Bob Woolmer, Basil d'Oliveira, Phil Russell and Ian Buxton to help me – but unless the keeper can rely on the unselfishness of a couple of team-mates, he should stay out of the nets.

I'll give you now a few practices to try out if you don't go into the nets. All you need is a friend, patience, determination, a bat and a ball (in some cases, a golf or tennis ball will do). The first one needs a couple of stumps or jackets. Place them five yards apart and stand in the middle in the crouch position with your gloves on. Get your mate to throw the ball anywhere in that five-yard area and then we'll see how good you are at diving to retrieve the ball, throwing it back and getting into position again quickly. The thrower should be about five yards away, and as your reactions sharpen up he can come nearer.

Then your friend can knock a cricket ball at you with one hand. You need a strong arm for this (Norman Gifford's very good at it) because you have to hold the bat one-handed as you toss the ball onto it. The keeper should throw the ball back to his mate's hand, *not* to the bat, because the keeper needs time to check his gloves are on properly and also to get into a half-crouch position. He should be four or five yards away from the bat, and again it's a great way

35

to quicken reactions and give you a sight of the ball.

Here's another one with a friend. Stand four yards from a wall and facing it. Get the other chap to stand a yard behind you. He can then throw the ball without you realizing where it's being directed. All you can do is crouch, anticipate and intercept as soon as it rebounds off the wall. It could be coming through your legs, over your shoulder or either side at any height. This again helps reactions and really makes you concentrate, and when you start to do well at this one, stand nearer to the wall. Start with a tennis ball and then graduate to a golf ball – after a small white golf ball the red cricket cherry will seem reassuringly large.

Another one with a tennis or golf ball that you can do on your own. Stand five yards away from the wall, throw the ball on the ground onto the wall and try to gather it cleanly. You don't need gloves for this one, it can be done in a garage or indoors, but the ground surface must be hard.

One practice that the keeper should never forget about is high catching. Many do forget about this – it's almost as if they never expect to have to sprint twenty yards or so with their eyes glued to the ball, shouting, 'Mine'. A team-mate should throw or hit a ball as high as possible and then the keeper should never look down or away when running for the catch. They really can be nerve-racking ones to take in a game, and I well remember two I dropped. One was at Adelaide against South Australia with Mike Denness's team. Bob Causby top-edged a hook off Chris Old, it went straight up in the air, I shouted, 'Mine', and set off twenty yards and then a couple more past the crease. I was keeping my eye on the ball in best textbook fashion until the very last second, when I saw the non-striking batsman Ashley Woodcock bearing down on me. Instead of veering to one side he deliberately ran straight at me. I took my eye off the ball for a crucial instant, it missed the gloves, hit my shoulder and I ended up flat on my back like a schoolboy. Keith Fletcher appealed at first slip for obstruction of the field, but I was too annoyed at my own lapse to care.

That was the first time in first-class cricket that I'd dropped a skier. The second time was at Edgbaston against Warwickshire.

Alvin Kallicharran skied one towards backward point, I claimed it, but backward point shouted at the same time. I thought I was going to run into him, took my eye off the ball, and it fell a yard in front of me. The crowd loved it, but I was furious at myself.

It was pleased with one skier I took, though. It was in a Benson and Hedges match with Gloucestershire. Mike Procter was looking dangerous at a crucial stage in the game when he slogged one in the air off Eddie Barlow and it went swirling over my head. I was standing back ten yards, and I had to turn two full circles behind me to get the ball because it was spinning so much. My heart was really pounding, but I kept my eye fixed on the ball and took it. I watched the catch again on a video belonging to the Gloucester coach Graham Wiltshire, and I was pleased with it.

In club and school cricket I've seen some comical dropped skiers, but all I can advise the keeper is to claim everything round the wicket, shout clearly as soon as you can, and just don't get distracted, not even for a second.

So the keeper's doing his body exercises and he's practising hard. Now it's time for the running programme. Solid running up and down hills builds up vital power in the thighs – but don't rush it because you could put too much strain on your Achilles tendons. Stamina running's not so important for a keeper as it is for a fast bowler, but at Derbyshire Eddie Barlow initiated a winter's training schedule that made us the fittest side in the championship. For the first winter we all had to run three miles daily in twenty-two minutes, and he also wanted fifty press-ups, fifty squat thrusts and the same amount of front curls. The next winter it was three miles in twenty minutes and double the press-ups, etc. Each time Eddie was fitter than anyone when he returned from abroad – a year older than me, he'd watch my progress and work hard to be fitter. It was great competition, and there's no doubt it made my job as keeper easier because our lads were far better in the field.

The attitude to fitness among county players is very different from when I started in 1960. I was a part-time professional footballer and fairly fit, but the ones over thirty hadn't a hope. Yet now at my age I've got to be as fit as players on the staff who're nearly twenty years younger. A few years back the only fit ones at the start of the season were the pro footballers. In the first week, we'd train with the medicine ball in the mornings, have some fielding practice and then go home. In the second week it was fielding in the morning and nets in the afternoon, and then most of the players would just rely on match play to get them fit. No wonder the Australians and the South Africans always outclassed us in the field in those days. Not any more though . . .

During the winter at home, I'll run daily for three quarters of an hour near my home. I'll do twenty-yard sprints up and down the hills, run on a slight slope for about a mile, then jog gently down and go back up again for about a quarter of a mile about three times. Then I'll choose a very steep gradient which I walk up. All this builds up strength in the calves and thighs.

I never run on roads or any hard surfaces. That constant pounding jars the knees – as I know to my cost. A week before going on Ray Illingworth's tour to Australia, I had a terrible pain in one of my knees. The Stoke City physiotherapist examined me and said I had fluid on the knee and was never to run again on hard surfaces. I daren't tell Ray Illingworth about my injury, so on the thirty-hour flight to Australia I sat with my leg fully extended with a crepe bandage from the top of the thigh to halfway down the calf. It soon cleared up, but I'd never have forgiven myself if I'd missed my first official England tour because of road running.

A word of encouragement to the keeper who's just starting to take his skills more seriously and wants to improve: don't cheat on all these exercises. If you're training on your own, you've just go to push yourself. Don't imagine it's all going to make you a super athlete, but it *will* make you a better wicketkeeper. Don't think, 'I don't fancy that exercise, I've done enough for today'; be your own conscience, push yourself as a matter of pride. Otherwise you'd be as well sitting in the armchair . . .

And don't kid yourself that you can eat anything you like provided you do enough training. Good nourishing food is

38

another way of improving your performance on the field, because as Rod Marsh found out in his first series for Australia, a fat keeper isn't a good one. If you're big round the waist you're simply not agile, and I know county keepers who lack the will-power to refuse a second roll and butter and then can't understand why their wicketkeeping doesn't improve. I know I'm lucky because I'm naturally slim, but I also know I must stay away from most fatty foods and cakes. I train myself during the day to refuse fatty foods because I know at the end of the day's play I'll have a good nourishing steak. In the morning I'll have a substantial breakfast (egg, bacon and tomato, piece of toast and honey, one cup of tea with one sugar), because it then sets me up for the day. I'll have a cup of tea at the ground before play starts, and during the lunch and tea intervals I'll just have a cheese roll and a cup of tea. I'm really scared stiff of putting on weight – I've been 10 stone 7 lb since I started with Derbyshire, and I don't want to see it alter.

The big dietary problem for club cricketers is drink – and I sympathize. I like a pint after a match just as much as anybody, but if you play the game for a living and your role in the team demands peak fitness, you just can't abuse your body for too long. It's different for a club player – he's worked hard at his job all week, he looks forward to a few pints with the lads after the match. But he should stop and imagine what he'll look like at forty-five and try to cut down without being miserable about it. And if you drink *before* a game, you can't have much pride in your role as the wicketkeeper of your side. Yet you can still have fun after the game without knocking back ten pints, especially on an empty stomach.

Even if the keeper's a conscientious one who doesn't get too boozed, trains as hard as he can and practises well, he can still come unstuck with injury. And it's difficult and frustrating for a keeper, because he can't carry an injury in the same way as a batsman or a slow bowler. There's an element of selfishness to consider, because the keeper may have just got into the school first eleven or the top club side in the area and doesn't want to stand down for someone who could easily keep his place. It all depends on the state of the game, your captain's attitude and the pain you're suffering – but don't play the hero just for the sake of it. If you're in a lot of pain, you won't be concentrating too well and may easily let the side down.

There's a pain barrier to go through, and it varies at all levels and with different types. I've seen some right fuddy-duddies in county sides who convince themselves they're badly injured, then spend most of their time on the treatment table for trivial injuries and do very little for the side. It's an attitude of mind, and anyone can be fitter and more reliable if he tells himself so.

I've seen some great displays of courage on the cricket field in my time – none more so than from that fine leg-spinner Intikhab Alam in Australia. We were playing at Adelaide for the Rest of the World against Australia in an unofficial Test. Two days before the match started, Inty had been in bed with a heavy cold, and on the first day we fielded he sent down fifteen eight-ball overs in a hundred-degree temperature. At the end of the day's play we all sat in the dressing room having a drink, and Inty, who was terribly dehydrated, sat on a couch for an hour and a half. He then tried to get up, but was hit by the most terrible cramp. Poor Inty was in awful pain. He just couldn't move, and he had to spend the night in an Adelaide hospital. I've never seen anyone so stiff – yet he bowled the next day! It was a remarkable performance, and I really admired his resilience.

Nobody's suggesting you should be a hero just for the sake of it, but if you *do* keep yourself fit and resilient, you've got a fine chance of being a good wicketkeeper. Mind you, there are plenty of other things to master as well . . .

4 Standing Back

In my book it's a sin to drop a normal catch when you're standing back to a fast bowler. I believe a competent close catcher can do the job. The difficult takes down the leg side are another question, but with the catches you can see all the way from the edge of the bat, it should be a matter for self-disgust if they plop out.

The principles involved are fairly straightforward – good footwork, keeping the eye on the ball, concentration and calmness. But first you have to judge where to stand for the fast bowler. Eventually this becomes instinctive, but you must be in a position to take the ball waist-high, not ankle- or shoulder-high, when standing back. It all depends on the pace of the wicket and the bowler's speed. If you're playing in a school or club match and you don't know a thing about a new seam bowler who's just been brought on, then err on the side of caution at the start. Stand about twelve yards back, watch his run up and see what effort he puts into his action. Don't get too ambitious at the start because he may take a few overs to get warmed up. Better to take the ball down by the ankles early on, than have to grab it as it's sailing past your shoulder.

The furthest I've stood back is about twenty-five yards – to my former Derbyshire colleague Alan Ward, to Bob Willis both home and abroad, and to John Snow when he really slipped himself in Australia under Ray Illingworth. For Dennis Lillee it was about twenty-two yards back, but in my career the two fastest have been Willis and Ward.

The exact places to stand when taking a fast bowler are fairly

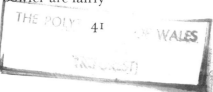

obvious, but in one respect I differ from most keepers. With a right-hand bowler and a right-hand bat – the most common situation – I'll stand behind the stumps rather than just outside the line of the off stump. I think that if the batsman gets an outside edge it's easier to get to the right from my position. If you're behind the stumps you can cover both sides, although you've got to go that much further for the outside edge, so you have to back your agility. And my stance doesn't affect my vision when the right-hand bowler's coming over the wicket – the most common position.

The biggest vision problem for a keeper standing back is with a left-arm bowler like John Lever coming over the wicket to a right-hand bat. Then you must go wider – say past first slip's position. This has one advantage – it saves one slip, and the skipper can then use just two slips and a gulley. Legside takes in this situation are difficult. You've got so much more ground to cover if the batsman glances it fine. So you've got to watch the bowler's arm and anticipate the ball sooner. Don't wait for the ball to pitch: train your eye so that you're on your way while the batsman's shaping for the glance. Sounds difficult, I know, but the legside catches to a fast bowler are very satisfying ones. One of the best ones I've taken was given not out. It was against Jamaica, and with the first ball of the match Lawrence Rowe glanced Geoff Arnold off the face of the bat. I anticipated it well, dived and caught it one-handed. The umpire didn't see the shot, Geoff Arnold had to be restrained by Mike Denness, Rowe went on to make a hundred, and on the strength of that knock he made 302 in the third Test.

My best catch standing back? It was off Mike Smith, the Middlesex opener, with Mike Hendrick bowling. He was bowling right arm over, the right-hand bat got a thick inside edge, and I caught it one-handed down the leg side after changing direction. I'd been going down the offside, but the bat was so far away from his body that the inside edge didn't hit his pads. I was pleased because I had to change direction for a very fast nick, and because my concentration was good.

Mention of Mike Hendrick reminds me of a little ploy we'd worked out that baffled the England close-in fielders. For several seasons Mike had been perfecting an occasional slow off-cutter to get the batsman playing early. It worked well with Derbyshire and we tried it for the first time in a Test against New Zealand at Trent Bridge. I could see how the ball was wrapped in Mike's hand as he ran in, and proceeded to walk five yards towards the batsman. Mike Brearley and the other slips couldn't believe their eyes, but my reasons were simple. If the batsman had played too soon at the off-cutter and edged it to me, it would have fallen short of my normal position to Hendrick – fifteen yards back. So with the ball coming slowly onto the bat I had to move nearer to the stumps for the glance or outside edge.

The biggest problem with standing back is just when to go for catches that are going towards first and second slip. The dilemma is obvious: do you let the ball go to the slips and see it spilled when you could've perhaps caught it better with the gloves, do you dive for anything at the risk of robbing a better-placed slip of a simple catch, or do you decide against going for the snick only to see the ball fall short of the slips? There's no point in saying to yourself, 'I could've dived forward and got that one,' when it's too late. You must always go for the snick instantly once you've made up your mind. Don't hesitate, because with a fast bowler that split-second delay makes all the difference. In my book it's a crime to start to go for a catch and then chicken out. I realize it's a matter of experience and instinct over judging whether to go for it – but there's no rule of thumb about the right moment. You've just got to trust your luck and be positive. Anticipation's the key. You must be expecting every ball to be nicked, so that you're halfway there when it happens. And once you're committed – *go all the way*.

I like my first slip to stand a little wider than normal so that ideally we won't impede each other. Try to tell yourself it's a lack of confidence in your ability if the first slip stands near to you. Define your diving area and try to command it.

One Test catch that pleased me was off Sadiq Mohammad. Bob Willis was bowling, and because Sadiq's a left-hander I had

PAGES 44–9 *Three examples of keepers' catches in that 'no-man's-land' between him and first slip. Each time, the keeper realizes in a split thousandth of a second that the ball won't go straight to slip and that he must go all the way for it. No half-measures . . . dive if necessary, and do it one-handed if there's no alternative. The successful keeper here is myself (New Zealand's Stephen Boock off Bob Willis' bowling)*

*Success here for Rod
Marsh (England's Keith
Fletcher off Max Walker)*

A great catch by Alan Knott (Australia's Rick McCosker off Tony Greig)

to stand wide on the off for the right-hand bowler. He edged the one that was going away from him, and I took it near Graham Roope's right foot at second slip. I was pleased because I saw it all the way, went for the catch instantly and got both hands to the ball. And I'm not sure if it would have reached Graham Roope.

There were a few more in the two series over here against New Zealand and Pakistan that may have looked good on television as I dived in front of first slip, but I didn't find them all that special. My best catch of that Test summer was one that probably didn't look special at all. The New Zealand tail-ender Brendon Bracewell edged Bob Willis off a full-length ball outside the off stump. The length was so full that it was never more than four feet off the ground. I dived in front of Mike Brearley at first slip and caught it one-handed. From a technical point of view it was very satisfying because the ball came through fast and low.

I took a similar catch in a Test in Pakistan. Again Sadiq was the batsman and Willis the bowler. It was a full-length, fast ball outside the off stump, Sadiq dropped his bat down hard on it, and it came through inches off the ground. I didn't have to dive, but the ball came through so low that my glove brushed the ground as I held it.

Sometimes the ball just sticks and everyone says, 'What a great catch,' when you know very well it was all a matter of luck. I've caught Warwickshire's Geoff Humpage twice in Benson and Hedges Cup matches when there was no slip and I had to dive or leap a long way. It looks spectacular and you must keep your eye on the ball, but many times the ball will stay in the gloves for no real reason other than that it's your lucky day.

The keeper also has other important roles to play when standing back. Because he should be an inspiration to the rest of the side, he should be reading the game and letting the batsman know he's around. When a run's being taken, you must get up to the stumps as quickly as possible, especially in limited-over matches where the batsman's trying for a run off every ball. This is where the keeper's got to be fit, when he's rushing around all over the place and the wild returns are zooming in. If you are fit and do all this, you

OPPOSITE *A catch that pleased me technically because the snick kept low and I had to dive in front of Mike Brearley at first slip. The bowler is Bob Willis and the batsman Brendon Bracewell of New Zealand*

won't have to think about it and you'll still be able to concentrate.

If there's one thing that annoys me in all grades of cricket, it's when the batsmen can steal an overthrow because of sloppiness. I want fielders to back me up in case of overthrows, and I also see it as my job to make sure the ball gets into the bowler's hand as he's walking back to his mark. Even when the ball's been played away and there hasn't been a run, I'll watch it being lobbed to the bowler before I turn my back on him. There's often chaos in club or school cricket when the ball goes over the bowler's head, so remember that the batsmen are perfectly entitled to the extra run and watch the ball all the time to make sure they don't get it. Train yourself to move a couple of yards towards the stumps even if there's no chance of a run – it's always nice to let the batsmen know he's dealing with an alert wicketkeeper who won't allow anything slack.

Awkward legside takes off fast bowlers also sort out the keepers; you can be made to look a right fool as you dive over the ball or it goes over your gloves, or past your right hand when you've gone too far. You must try to get the body behind the ball, keep your hands together and the pads behind the gloves as a second line of defence in case the ball squirts out. Keep your head over the ball. Don't even think of getting injured. If your head's down, your body will be leaning forward and you'll automatically be in a better position for the take. It's amazing how many county and Test keepers I've seen who occasionally forget fundamentals like moving the feet for a legside take. I see them taking the ball about a yard down the leg side with their hands away from the body. If they'd anticipated properly, their bodies would be across and in line with the ball, so they wouldn't need to rely on spectacular last-ditch dives that may impress the spectators but are technically bad. Always try to get two hands to the ball, and leave the flashy stuff until it's really necessary.

Have pride in your work behind the stumps; be furious with yourself if you let any byes through. When standing back to reasonably fast bowlers, there's no real reason why you should allow any byes. Lack of concentration's often the reason. I always

Those awkward low ones down the leg side off the fast bowler can make the keeper look silly. Keep your head down, get the body over the ball, keep the hands together even though it's a wide ball, and don't even think about the ball hitting you in the face. Get everything behind the ball – in this case I've got my right pad behind the gloves as a precautionary measure

know exactly how many byes I've lost – I was proud that 1500 runs had been scored against Ray Illingworth's side in Australia with me behind the stumps before a bye was lost, and I was annoyed when the first byes came, because they should have been wides! It was against South Australia, and Bob Willis sprayed one down the leg side that swung even more after it passed the stumps. I hadn't a hope of getting a glove on the ball – I wasn't within three yards of it – but the umpire signalled four byes rather than wides. I couldn't believe it, because my proud record had gone in such a silly way. Afterwards the umpire, himself a former keeper, apologized to me and said he was wrong!

It may sound fanatical to worry about such things, but the keeper's the one who has to drive himself. He must set targets and tell himself he owes it to the side to keep a clean sheet. When I made my second appearance for England after a gap of seven years I was determined to put on a good display . . . and that included no byes. Well I let one bye through in Pakistan's total of 407, but I was even annoyed at that solitary bye, because it came from a sloppy legside take by me when I went to get a ball from Chris Old with my left hand to save my injured right one. I should have ignored the injury, concentrated harder and remembered to use two hands whenever possible.

I've had the pleasure of keeping to some great fast bowlers around the world, but none rates higher than Dennis Lillee. To me he was the complete pace bowler – hostile, fast, subtle, accurate, a master of his craft. I'll never forget keeping to him at Johannesburg when the International Wanderers played a South African team including Richards, Pollock, Barlow, Rice and Lee Irvine as batsmen. Dennis had arrived only a few days before the match and he still wasn't acclimatized in the first innings. He was pasted to the tune of nought for sixty, and the crowd, who were well aware of his reputation, gave him some stick. In the final innings the South Africans needed 260 to win – a doddle on a good wicket and with so many fine batsmen. Well, Dennis took 7 for 23 and brushed them aside. His dander was up, his pride was at stake, and he was magnificent that day.

Also on that tour we played a game at Benoni with the members of our party opposing each other to make the sides equal. Out come Mike Denness and Greg Chappell to open, and our skipper, Glenn Turner, has a word with Dennis. Turner comes back to first slip and says to me, 'He won't have a fine leg and he only wants two on the leg side. All he'd say was that he wouldn't bowl down the leg side.' And he didn't – not one stray ball in six overs. It was perfect line-and-length high-speed bowling on or just outside the off stump, an amazing display, especially as he was bowling against one of the great on-side batsmen in Greg Chappell.

With a bowler like Dennis Lillee, a keeper's job is easy. But the real fun and challenge comes when you have to stand up at the stumps . . .

5 Standing up to the Stumps

The real test of a wicketkeeper comes when he has to show how good are his reactions, hands and anticipation when standing up. A lot of judges see this purely in relation to slow bowlers, but in my opinion it applies to medium-pacers and sometimes even fast bowlers.

On rare occasions it's tactically necessary to stand up to the quickies; it happened with me in Pakistan when Javed Miandad was going down the wicket to John Lever and scuffing up the wicket deliberately so Pakistan's slow bowlers could take advantage of a worn wicket the next day. It was my biggest challenge of that tour, because John Lever's pretty sharp, and with his left-arm slant across the right-hand batsman I had to look nippy on many occasions, especially with the ball keeping so low. I was pleased with my performance because I caught Miandad when he chopped Lever down hard and I caught the under edge just outside the off stump.

While standing up to Lever at Karachi in that Pakistan series I made the best stumping of my career – but it was given not out. Miandad was again roughing up the wicket, so I stood up to John. He sent one down the leg side, Miandad tried to swing it through mid-wicket, played it on the walk, missed it and his back foot went forward. I had the bails off like a flash, and he was still out of his crease when they landed on the ground. Yet the umpire said, 'Not out' – and I was so angry that Bob Willis at leg slip had to restrain me. It seemed so unfair, because we'd worked that legside ploy to dismiss a top-class player but the umpire hadn't noticed a thing.

When I first started with Derbyshire I had a bit of an inferiority

55

complex about standing up to the fast men. I'd seen some fine keepers in Minor Counties cricket doing it, and I thought I should be the same. But I worked out that I'd miss far more edges standing up than take legside stumpings off a quick bowler, so I thought it best to be safe. Yet I've done it when I thought it necessary – I remember stumping Leicestershire's Brian Booth off Brian Jackson after spotting that Booth was standing two yards out of his crease every ball, trying to get Jackson to drop short so that he could pull him. And once when Farokh Engineer danced down the track and pulled Peter Eyre for a mid-wicket four, I stood up to threaten him. Sure enough the Lancashire keeper swung once too often and I got my stumping.

It's very satisfying to stump someone off a fast bowler, but be careful. It may seem daring and clever to do it but you can be made to look an idiot. Even if the ball's coming through low, it's best to stand back because you'll have more time to sight the grubber. You've really got to be able to trust the accuracy and intelligence of your bowler if you decide to stand up, so don't be foolhardy, remember the rest of the team if you fancy an ego trip.

But you should *want* to stand up to the medium-pace bowlers. It should be a matter of pride: do you want to remain a stopper or do you want to improve? If you're breathing down his neck it'll make the batsman play differently – he won't be so keen to go down the wicket. And if you pick up a stumping or two, the medium-pacers won't complain. But don't go straight into a club or school match determined to try it out. Try it out in the nets with your seamers, ask their advice and impress on them the need to bowl accurately. When I first started with Derbyshire, Ian Buxton was still bowling big inswingers. I worked it out and told him there were a few stumpings on the leg side going begging if I stayed back, because many batsmen play the mid-wicket shots on the walk. He agreed, and some of my best legside stumpings have been off Ian's bowling.

You must always be near enough to the stumps to break them without having to dive forward – this applies to both spin and seam bowling. Teach yourself to watch the ball from the bowler's

OPPOSITE *Not the ideal position for the legside take – but I was standing up to John Lever in a Test in Pakistan. The position of Javed Miandad's bat shows it was an inswinging yorker from the left-handed bowler, so strictly speaking I should have that right leg across for extra protection if the ball whips through low. But with a bowler of Lever's pace I don't have the time to get into the ideal position, though at least I've got my left leg behind the gloves as a back-up. Shortly after this picture was taken I stumped Miandad off Lever, the best stumping of my career. Unfortunately the umpire was asleep at the time, so he was given not out* hand, and then as soon as you see that the ball's going down the leg side, get across as soon as possible so that you're outside the line of the ball with your body slanted in towards the stumps for the possible stumping. Keep the hands together and at knee height when going to the leg side because that position will make the rest of your body remain low – the head and shoulders particularly.

You must keep the head down. If you lose sight of the ball

Look at Alan Knott's hands – he's in a brilliant position and his hands haven't followed Ian Chappell's legside swing. Alan's gloves are still just outside the off stump, because that's where the ball pitched, and if Chappell edges that's where the ball will go. Alan's body is well forward, and if there's a chance of a stumping he's in the ideal position

you're struggling for the stumping or the catch because it can deviate at the last moment. I've seen Test keepers like Rodney Marsh turn their heads away when the ball's coming down the leg side – that's not good wicketkeeping. You should never think about getting hit when standing up . . . in all my time in the game standing up I've only picked up a couple of stitches in the chin when a ball from Edwin Smith hit the stumps and came in my face.

How not to take the ball when it's going down the leg side. Australia's Rod Marsh has ignored one of the cardinal rules of wicketkeeping: he's taken his eyes off the ball, and if it pops up for a dolly catch or there's a stumping chance he won't look too clever. This was always one of Rod's big faults – strange really, considering he was such a tough customer. If you watch the ball and ignore the swishing bat, I assure you there's little chance of getting hit

The right and the wrong way to use the gloves when standing up. I hope Derryck Murray of the West Indies doesn't mind me pointing out that his hands should be together – otherwise, if Greg Chappell snicks one, he'll have to adjust rapidly. And I'm glad to see the camera's caught me in the right position standing up against Geoff Howarth – note my right little finger keeping my gloves together

The big problem with taking inswingers while standing up to a right-hand batsman is that you lose sight of the ball for a few seconds when the batsman's body obscures your view. That's when you really must concentrate, keep your head, and with instinct and a little luck, find the line of the ball. That's why legside stumpings are so satisfying – there was one for me against Western Australia for the England touring team which gave Geoff Boycott, of all people, a rare wicket. Chadwick played the walking shot to a leg-stump ball, it was obscured for a moment, but I got the right line. I was very pleased, although Geoff Boycott was so used to the professionalism of his county keeper, Jimmy Binks, that he didn't seem at all surprised.

I think one legside stumping had a big influence on my going on that particular Australian tour under Ray Illingworth. I stumped Colin Cowdrey off a Buxton inswinger, and Colin said, 'Well stumped, Bob,' before walking away. Colin was the vice-captain to Ray Illingworth, and I think had a lot to do with my selection a few weeks later.

I've got happy memories of that day against Kent, because I dismissed three international batsmen in one afternoon standing up to the seamers. There was Cowdrey, then Mike Denness off Phil Russell, then I stumped Asif Iqbal as he went down the wicket to Peter Eyre. The Denness dismissal was the best because the ball bounced quickly off the shoulder of his bat on the off side and I hung on to it at an awkward angle.

These offside catches standing up are difficult because you have to watch the ball all the time and then react very quickly to take what are, in effect, catches to first slip. And often your gloves are tucked up above your right shoulder when taking the catch and you can find yourself in an awkward position. Another catch of this type that pleased me was when I stood up to Bob Woolmer in a Test trial and caught Tony Lewis high up after he'd played forward and edged the ball. They may look simple catches, but believe me, you need a bit of luck for them.

Legside stumpings 'through the gate' are very difficult. That's when the ball from a right-hander passes through the bat and pad, misses the leg stump and makes the keeper look a right Charlie as he fumbles the chance because he thought the ball was going to hit the wicket. They can be a nightmare, but in one county game against Worcestershire I was lucky enough to get three of these stumpings – all off the same bowler, Ian Buxton. Each time the batsman played with the bat well away from the body, the ball went through bat and pad and again I was obscured for a few seconds. The important thing is to train yourself not to take the ball till it's past the stumps. Assume it won't hit the stumps and always be ready to spring into action.

The best medium-pacer I've kept to was Basil d'Oliveira. He was a very intelligent, underrated bowler, always varying his pace and line and able to bowl a particular delivery at will if you were trying for a stumping. He had an unflappable temperament, and it was one of my greatest thrills to keep to Dolly on Ray Illingworth's tour because to me he'd been almost a godlike figure for his behaviour and dignity since coming over from South Africa. And when I managed a stumping and a catch off his bowling in New South Wales, I was walking on air.

So much for medium-pacers. The real art of keeping wicket, though, is dealing with the spinners. It's more physically demanding than with any other pace because there's little time to relax between deliveries. Yet it's much more stimulating. I get more pleasure keeping to slow bowling than from any other facet of my job, especially when the wicket's turning and you expect to be involved with every ball. It's marvellous keeping to an intelligent bowler pitting his wits against a great batsman because you're near enough to appreciate the batsman's footwork and speed of reaction and the bowler's control and cunning. The demands of concentration are greater as well – there's so little time to react that you tell yourself that every long hop, every full toss is coming smack into your gloves. And the self-discipline is demanding; you must train yourself to keep crouched down until the slow bowler's delivery has nearly pitched, otherwise you'll be in position too soon and won't be able to adjust quickly. Staying down long enough is the difference between the ball going into the middle of the gloves or taking the tips of the fingers and plopping out.

When crouching down for the slow bowler, I have my hands outside the line of the bat on the off side, so that if there's a deflection from the edge, the ball will hopefully go straight into the gloves rather than force you to move the hands hurriedly for a ball that's leaving you. Many keepers have their hands right behind the bat, but I feel this leads to snatching – don't forget you've got a split second to go for the snick, and you should always be aiming to get both gloves behind the ball. To keep my hands cupped together as often as possible, I have my right little finger overlapping the left little finger. I'm right-handed, so that when the ball comes to me it'll come into my right hand first. That's particularly useful for legside stumpings, because you can do them so much quicker with one hand, especially if it's your favourite hand. With a keeper like George Sharp of Northants a legside stumping's more difficult because he's naturally left-handed so he must find it more awkward than me.

Let's take the keeper's position for the off-spinner bowling to the right-hander, a testing position because the keeper's view will often be obscured as the ball turns away to leg. For this one, I'll crouch with my left foot just behind the middle stump and my hands outside the off peg. When the off-break's bowled outside the off stump, the batsman will be playing for the turn to leg and my hands will be waiting for the edge on the outside, so they won't necessarily move towards the stumps at the start. So if he does edge it on the off – which is the most common one – the ball will come straight into my gloves and I won't have to dive back towards the off and take a chance.

But you've got to be ready to go back towards the stumps in a flash – and a catch I once took off Geoff Miller proves the point. Graham Johnson of Kent drove at an off-break without using his feet. The bat was a long way from the body and I stayed inside the line of the ball for the inside edge. Sure enough it came, hard and fast, but I was in position for it. What was technically satisfying about the catch was that I'd realized that with Johnson driving two feet outside the off stump I wouldn't have got anywhere near the outside edge. It would have been a sharp chance to slip's right hand if anything, so I backed my judgement and it worked.

You really have to train your eye to expect a stumping off a slow bowler. There are ways of telling if there's a chance of one – if a batsman's getting tied down, he'll be itching to hit the ball over the top or to use his feet. You can tell if he's tensed up and frustrated by his facial muscles or if his feet are tapping too much – and in club or school cricket this will be even more evident, because there aren't so many calm bluffers at the crease as in first-class cricket. So keep an eye on the batsman and maintain your concentration. Don't forget to stay down till the ball's nearly pitched, and if you then sense it's going down the leg side, chassis across swiftly. To do this I click my right heel once against the left heel. This helps to activate me, keeps my on my toes. Don't forget to have your head at stump height when waiting for the delivery and when it's time to chassis across, keep the head down, the hands just below the knee, arms extended, shoulders down and the body weight forward. If you're down low for as long as possible, you've got a far better chance of getting to the ball – especially when it skids through low.

When taking down the leg side, don't worry about the textbook recommendation that the left toe should be pointing back towards the stumps as you're swinging the hands back to the leg stump. If you *feel* natural, do it your way – as long as you can break the wicket without having to dive. And wherever possible, keep the hands together from the moment the bowler comes in to when the ball's returned to him. Quite simply, two hands are better than one in most cases, and it increases your chances of hanging on to the ball. Try to avoid being flashy just for the sake of it.

A word on the crouch position. Many old-timers didn't bother with the crouch, they'd just bend halfway down so they could be in position for the high catch. I've tried this in the nets and I find it far more difficult to dive down and across. Surely you can spring across more easily when you're crouched low?

How can you tell where the off-spinner's going to pitch the ball?

I'm pleased with my position here. Pakistan's Haroon Rashid has already driven the ball, but I'm still crouched low, watching the ball, with my hands still pointing down. After a time you get into a groove when keeping wicket, and provided you keep your concentration, the principles that have been coached into you should work automatically

OVERLEAF *How to stand up when the batsman's stretching forward. In this case I've been partly unsighted by New Zealand's John Wright, but I've kept my head and body down and my gloves pointing downwards so that I'm in position for the one that beats the bat or shoots through low. And if it bounces I can still get up quickly — whereas if I was standing taller, I would struggle to get down for the low ones*

*I'm delighted to say I'm
in the right position for a
legside take. Phil
Edmonds has bowled one
that was going down the
leg side and Geoff
Howarth's played it away
safely, but I was ready
for a stumping or the fine
tickle. The head and body
are still down low, the
hands are below the knee
for the skidding ball, and
my face tells you how
hard I'm concentrating*

With the county and Test keepers it's a matter of experience, instinct and the good, trained eye a professional sportsman needs. You learn to pick out the off-break, the one that goes straight on, the seamer and the outswinger by watching the ball through the air and the bowler's grip as he runs in. You get to know bowlers' little peculiarities – one may run up slightly differently, or turn the head away when he's getting into the delivery stride, and that way I'll know it's going to be an outswinger. The bowler and I never bother with signals – they trust me to spot the appropriate delivery.

Don't worry, you club and school keepers, it's unfair to expect you to spot such things. We play the game seven days a week, all round the world, and we should be able to back our judgement. In your case, I think it's best to work something out between the overs and expect the outswinger on, say, the fourth ball and the straight one for the second ball. And give the bowler a rocket if he forgets the sequence and sends you scuttling down the leg side when he bowls the outswinger!

The real test with an off-spinner comes when the wicket's sticky and the ball's standing up and nearly talking. That's when you have to pick the line up even more quickly and chassis across while watching the ball all the time. Those tricky ones that go through bat and pad are common on a sticky wicket, so keep concentrating. And with the bowler going round the wicket to improve his chances of an lbw decision, the keeper must stand a half-pace wider with the left foot on the off-stump area. So the loose one down the leg side will trouble the keeper when he's in this position – it's quickness of movement that's needed here rather than the ability to spot a particular type of delivery, because a good off-spinner will plug away on a sticky wicket, dropping it on or near the off stick, trying to get the ball to turn and bounce or getting the batsman to play for the turn that's not there so he'll edge it to the keeper or slip.

The off-spinner to the left-hand bat? That's easier because the ball's generally leaving the bat and the keeper can usually see it all the way. The principles are the same as for a right-hand bat.

73

Three facets of taking the off-spinner bowling to a left-hander. In (a) Geoff Miller's bowled a wide one outside the off stump, Warwickshire's Andy Lloyd has played and missed, and the ball's come right into my gloves. I was expecting a top edge here but I've kept my right foot in the proper position so I'm not too far away in the event of a possible stumping. I'm ready to take the ball back to the stumps, with my head and body still forward. In (b) I'm telling myself to stay down until the ball's pitched – that way I've got a far better chance of knowing where the ball's going. My feet are in a good position, with the right foot on the middle stump line and my head in range of the top of the bails. In (c) I've chassised across for a ball that's bounced slightly. Andy's turned it off his hips and I've stood up a little because of the extra bounce. But my gloves are still pointing downwards and I haven't gone too far across, so I'm still in a good stumping position if Andy had missed and overbalanced

(a)

(b)

(c)

A word on practising. Take one stump into a net and ask the off-spinner to bowl at you, with particular attention to the leg side. Then after you've got the feel of it, put a chair or a box in front of the stump, so you'll lose sight of the ball for a moment. Sometimes the off-break aimed at the middle stump will hit the object and you can see if you were in the right position, sometimes it'll come through to your gloves. Then ask a batsman to come into the nets and see how you shape up with his playing forward and your wondering where the ball's going to pitch. Practise hard, because it's great fun when you can stand up confidently at the stumps, knowing you're making a good stab at a difficult part of your job.

There aren't so many problems keeping to a leg-spinner and a right-hand bat. There are no vision difficulties, and because a leg-spinner's normally less accurate than an off-spinner he's more likely to lapse in length than direction. So you'll expect to take a few long hops and full tosses rather than do so much scampering down the leg side. With the googly, you should be able to spot it coming out of the back of his hand and then you can treat it as an off-break. So get ready for a legside take or a stumping 'through the gate'. Expect loose bowling from the leg-spinner and never forget that full tosses are difficult to take. Concentrate hard – many times a keeper thinks, 'That's going to be smashed,' when the batsman gets excited and edges the long hop or full toss. And remember the next ball after the long hop could be an absolute beauty that'll beat the batsman all ends up . . . and you too.

With a slow left-arm spinner, the keeper can again see the ball all the way when a right-hand bat's at the crease. He'll bowl four types – the orthodox leg-break, the 'arm' ball that's like an inswinger, the 'chinaman' (left-armer's off-break) and the quicker one that goes straight on and often turns out to be a yorker. With the quicker one it's even more vital to keep down till the last possible moment, because it could easily skid through ankle-high and the batsman may be taken by surprise by a full-length yorker, miss it and give you a possible stumping.

My normal stance is outside the off stump following the line of the ball but still close enough to the off stump to rock back for a possible stumping. Keep the pads together behind the gloves as a second line of defence so that if the ball skids through, the pads will stop the byes.

For a slow left-armer bowling to a left-hand bat, it's the same as an off-spinner to the right-hander: the right foot on the middle, and watch for the one that goes straight on.

The great thing about keeping to slow bowling is hatching plans and seeing them work. It's two against one – you and the bowler against the batsman – and it's marvellous to pit your wits. In the county game there are players like Neil Abberley, David Steele and Mike Smith of Middlesex who tend to fall over when playing in front of the wicket on the leg side. Then I'll say to Geoff Miller or Fred Swarbrook, 'Shove one down the leg side,' and I'm ready for the stumping. But the keeper who amazed me in his planning was John Murray whenever his Middlesex colleague Fred Titmus was bowling his off-spinners. Many times when I've batted against them, Murray's been in a legside position before Titmus has even bowled! Obviously this ploy had brought them many a stumping and it shows how much Murray could rely on the famous Titmus accuracy.

Don't snatch at a stumping – wait for the ball to come to you. In this case, Geoff Miller bowled a slower one down the leg side, Pakistan's Haroon Rashid swished at it, and although I was partly unsighted I kept my head and waited for the ball to pass the stumps. Another example of the importance of concentration – train yourself to remain cool behind the stumps

The sheer pleasure of a stumping's hard to explain to a non-keeper. There was the time in 1973 when I stumped Alvin Kallicharran in a Prudential Trophy match for England. Derek Underwood, bowling round the wicket, sent one down the leg side, Alvin walked into a ball of full length, missed it, I took it ankle-high and stumped him. The England tour party for the West Indies was just about to be picked, and Geoff Boycott wandered over to me and said, 'That's got you on the trip to West Indies.' I made the trip and I often wonder if he was right . . .

Stumpings off the skidding, low deliveries are very gratifying because you have to watch the ball very closely. Phil Edmunds and I got Geoff Howarth of New Zealand out in the Prudential Trophy match at Old Trafford when Geoff tried to force a looping 'arm' ball. He missed, it pitched right up on the blockhole and I had him. Geoff had made it into a full toss by trying to force it on the leg side, and I'd kept my head and hands down for the ball when it skidded through.

Don't be afraid to try for the stumping if you think there's a chance. Here Mohsin Khan of Pakistan had gone for an off-drive (Graham Roope's self-defensive action just in front proves that) and missed. I thought he might overbalance in the shot and was ready for the possible stumping. But he just kept that foot in and was rightly given not out. Yet it was worth a try, not least to let the batsman know you're on your toes

Another satisfying one – Wasim Raja off Geoff Cope in Pakistan. Wasim, who's very quick on his feet, went down the track trying to hit another six, it really zipped through at ankle height outside the off stump, and he was gone. I was doubly pleased, not only because of my good position, but we were into the third day in the field, my longest-ever stretch, and my concentration hadn't slackened.

The best keeper to slow bowling in my time was my idol, Keith Andrew. He made it all look so simple, he was always in position, nothing was ever flamboyant and he kept for many years to one of the trickiest left-arm slow bowlers, George Tribe – he was a real box of tricks. Alan Knott was the runner-up. A lot of people thought Knotty wasn't too hot standing up, but I really rated him. He had a beautiful pair of hands, superb anticipation, stern concentration, and did a lot to make Derek Underwood a great bowler for both Kent and England.

Underwood is the best left-arm spinner I've ever kept to, and the best all-round spinner for that matter. He is always on the spot, doesn't have you rushing around wondering what is coming next, is always trying cunning little things, and is a marvellous trier, with a high morale. He'll tie good batsmen down on a perfect wicket, and when it turns and bounces he is simply unplayable. Bob Willis has often said Derek got him many wickets because his nagging length would make the batsmen desperate to get runs off Bob and they'd throw their wickets away at the other end.

I had the great pleasure of keeping to a couple of fine slow left-armers on tour to Australia with the Rest of the World. Bishen Bedi was all tantalizing flight, with great guile and patience, and didn't mind giving away some runs, while Norman Gifford was a typical English spin bowler. He'd push it through quickly, with a sharp 'arm' ball, but he couldn't adjust to the different needs of tight limited-over cricket and of county and Test cricket where flight is more desirable. Underwood, on the other hand, was a combination of Bedi and Gifford who could always bowl the right way for different types of cricket.

The best off-spinner for me was Fred Titmus: great variation, a good line, he could make it turn and bounce and bowled a lovely away floater to the right-hander. Fred always seemed to get me out when we played Middlesex – I remember one match when both times I played forward and thought I'd killed the spin, only to watch the ball roll back onto the stumps. Ray Illingworth wasn't far behind Titmus in my book, but Fred had more variety and Illy was that little bit slower and therefore slightly easier to hit.

Unfortunately I haven't had the pleasure of keeping to many leg-spinners because of the nature of our modern game, but the best was easily Intikhab Alam. On the Rest of the World tour to Australia he bowled beautifully; he'd turn the ball just enough to get the edge rather than beat the batsman all ends up, his variation (top-spinner, googly, leg-break) was very good, and he was very resilient. Inty was one of the bowlers involved in the match that gave me the greatest pleasure behind the stumps. It was when a D. H. Robins eleven beat the all-conquering West Indians at Eastbourne. We beat them by ten wickets, and Bedi, Inty and Mushtaq – two leggies and one slow left-armer – all bowled beautifully. I've never seen any of them bowl better than in that match, and I had the time of my life!

I'd love to see more slow bowlers in the game, because it's so enjoyable keeping to them. You're in the action all the time and the tactical situation's so fascinating. I just hope the tide will soon turn, because the habits of the first-class game affect the club and school grades. I see far too many kids running long distances and bowling medium pace, and I just wish they'd stop, think and use their brains to master the really satisfying art of slow bowling. After all, the more spinners in the game, the more fun for the wicketkeeper.

6 It's a Team Game

A wicketkeeper must never forget he's part of a team rather than its star turn. He's a vital part, of course, but a lot of his duties are the unselfish ones designed to get the best out of his side when they're fielding. He must always be on hand to help his captain or the bowlers, while at the same time being the orchestrator of the fielding performance.

Everything the keeper does reflects on the overall fielding standard. Cricketers are no different from office workers or factory hands, in that sometimes they wake up and think, 'Oh God, another day in the field, I'll really have to force myself.' Well, a good wicketkeeper will make the fielders try hard by geeing them up, inspiring by example and handing out a few rockets if necessary. He can make a fielding side look far better than it really is by taking a poor return on the full toss, saving byes and encouraging the fielders. Try to avoid sloppy overthrows when the return's a bad one; I've seen many a club keeper let a ball go through when it's only a yard wide because he doesn't see why he should dive around. This is one area where I think it's permissible to be spectacular. If an overthrow's likely, go for the dramatic dive, one-handed if necessary. It should be a matter of pride to get every throw into your gloves, and hopefully your display will make the fielders concentrate and get on their toes.

Never lob the ball short of a fielder or the bowler once you've taken the ball. It's so untidy to see the ball on the ground and the batsmen thinking about an overthrow, and whenever I see something like that I think about my former Derbyshire skipper,

Donald Carr. In my early days he'd give me a fearful rocket if ever my lobs dropped short, and I never forget the lesson. It's a sin to see a fast bowler have to twist and dive for the ball when he should be conserving his energy. I get very shirty about this when I'm behind the stumps – many times Eddie Barlow told me to take it easy after I'd bawled out one of our fielders for sloppiness. I'd get frustrated because the fielding side should make the batsman feel uncomfortable all the time, not let him think, 'This lot don't seem very lively.' Even when I watch club or Minor Counties cricket, I feel like shouting at the fielding side when they're sloppy; it's all so avoidable if the pride's there . . .

I'm often asked about the method of throwing the ball back to a fielder or bowler. I know how the questioner feels – you feel a fool when you try to lob it gracefully and it plops out too soon or too late and you have to grovel around after it when it's just a few feet in front of you. Believe me, I find it a problem as well, and I genuinely have to concentrate when I'm throwing it. I try to judge the distance and then practise it before the game, because if I'm not concentrating I'll lob it back short and feel a fool when I get an old-fashioned look from a fielder. I'll try to keep fielders on their toes by varying the line; sometimes I'll lob it out on the off side, sometimes to mid-wicket, then mid-on – just to make sure the fielders are still on their toes. Then I'll throw it hard and low to a man in the bat/pad position or in the gully to see if their reactions are still sharp. But remember, never turn your back on the ball until it's back in the bowler's hand.

I've often been very flattered when players and spectators talk to me about the ball disappearing into my gloves from a long throw without a sound. They say it must be because I've got a good pair of hands, and I tell them it's because of my marvellous Bertie Oldfield gloves. I was very embarrassed when Keith Fletcher and Colin Cowdrey remarked on this one day in a match in Australia. 'Isn't it the same with all the keepers?' I asked. 'No,' they said, 'often it's a thud.' Dennis Amiss has noticed this as well, but honestly I think it's only to do with giving with the hands at the right moment when the ball arrives. But if the fielders *are*

OPPOSITE *One occasion when it's permissible to use just one hand. In going for this high return from a fielder, I've got both feet off the ground and I'm stretching back – so I might not have caught the ball with both hands. Note that I'm still keeping my eyes on the ball*

83

impressed, don't disillusion them – if they admire you, they'll try harder in the field to meet your standards.

One thing I insist on from my fielders is backing up. When I'm standing back and there's a quick fielder like Derek Randall or Peter Kirsten in my side, I know there'll be occasions when I haven't a hope of getting up to the stumps in time if there's a chance of a run-out from an attempted single. I've got to be reading the game closely and shout, 'Back up,' to gulley or mid-wicket as I'm racing to the stumps. That's the hallmark of a good fielding side – one whose members support each other, and particularly support the wicketkeeper.

I always find that the moment when we take the field is a crucial one. I'll sprint out quickly, get the new ball from the umpire just to attune myself to it, and then get the slips gathered round me and throw it back and forth for a minute or two. I'll throw it underarm and hard and they'll shell it back into my gloves. Then once the game starts I'll clap my gloves together and keep encouraging the slips to expect a catch every ball. All the innings I'll badger away at them several times an over with remarks like, 'Come on, this one's coming to you.' I don't know just how much notice they take of me, but I feel it gees them up when a little lethargy might be creeping in.

Should the keeper captain the side? In my opinion, no. He should be the foreman on the field, the physical inspiration, the one who tries to keep things moving, while the skipper should be more detached and analytical. He has to be more diplomatic, while a keeper can shout, 'Pull your finger out,' to a lazy fielder. In my experience the mental strains of keeping wicket mean you can't spare the time for the stresses of captaincy. I skippered Derbyshire for a couple of seasons, and although many judges thought my form behind the stumps didn't suffer, I'm sure they were wrong. There were too many details both on and off the field to occupy my mind, and I couldn't give my best to my wicket-keeping. I realized that I wasn't helping the side if I was missing chances, and that you're no less of a team man if you're not skipper. One incident crystallized my problem – Phil Sharpe was

84

standing in his usual first slip position and I was a yard in front of him. Just as the bowler was coming in, Phil suggested moving a man close in. He didn't mean to distract me, it was a genuine tactical suggestion made too late, but I just wasn't ready for the next ball. Sure enough it was an outside edge, and I dropped a straightforward chance because my mind had been distracted.

The cares of captaincy must have had a lot to do with the sad decline of Wasim Bari behind the stumps for Pakistan. For years Alan Knott used to tell me how highly he rated Wasim, but in the two series I played against him he was disappointing. He didn't seem to be concentrating, he was letting the ball plop in and out of his gloves, and his overall dispirited air didn't do the side any favours in the field. I'm sure the captaincy was the main reason.

Tactically the keeper can do so much for his captain. He's in the best position of all to judge whether the ball's swinging or spinning, and he should never be afraid to make recommendations. He can correct a bowler's faults – because he's watching him run up, and he can see if he's opening up his body too soon and spraying it down the leg side, or if his head's lolling around or his foot's in the wrong position in the delivery stride. He can recommend an extra slip when he knows the ball's swinging away from the bat, or perhaps a leg slip if it's nipping back.

He's also in a unique position to judge the merit of an appeal for lbw. I find that bowlers appeal too much for lbw's when they're not in a good position to judge. Many times they're off balance after delivery and haven't seen where the ball's pitched. I won't appeal unless I think it's fair, and many times an umpire in first-class cricket will take the keeper's reaction into account before giving a decision. That's a good idea in my opinion, but sometimes the umpire's trust in the keeper's position leads to a bad decision. One was at Cardiff when Geoff Miller got a Glamorgan right-hander plumb lbw with his awayswinger. I didn't read it though, and I was outside the leg stump as the batsman tried to sweep – a fact that the umpire noticed. A former keeper himself, he grinned at me and said, 'Not out.' He didn't realize that sometimes a keeper makes mistakes and that his position shouldn't always be the decisive factor in an lbw decision.

I think schoolboys and club cricketers appeal too much, and although some of my colleagues get on to me about staying quiet, I'll only appeal when I think it's reasonable. But I don't mind a bit of kidology now and again. I don't do it too much because it might spoil my concentration, but I'm not averse to saying, 'Well bowled,' loudly enough for the batsman to hear when I know he's short of form and confidence. I occasionally tell tail-enders the ball's really turning just to get them worried, and if he's been in for a long time, I'll say loudly, 'Is the fast bowler warming up?' in the hope that he'll then have a slog or go down the wicket.

The keeper can use a bit of cunning when the batsman's turning for a comfortable second run. Just as he's grounded his bat at the bowler's end, he'll have his back to the ball and I'll shout, 'You've got him, John,' to the fielder. That'll make him hesitate, look for the ball in the field and perhaps refuse a certain run. I call that bluffing rather than gamesmanship because the batsman should really ignore me and trust his own judgement. But the keeper must know when to keep quiet. If it's a close one, keep quiet and concentrate on the ball coming in from the fielder.

In county cricket the wicketkeeper's in a great position to contribute to the county grapevine, that highly professional system whereby the defects of a batsman are analysed and assessed. The keeper can judge the batsman's strengths and weaknesses better than most, because he's at close quarters. It's really fascinating to pit your wits against a fine player who sooner or later realizes that natural ability's not enough to see him prosper in the game.

A chap like David Gower is a fine natural player, but he's only human and has his slight defects. Mike Hendrick fancies him in the gulley area because he doesn't quite get over his forcing shot in that region, something the New Zealanders realized by getting him caught a couple of times there. We'll place a man at backward point and gulley, then keep him quiet for a time with short-of-a-length bowling, then give him one outside the off stump and hope he'll slash at it. I've also noticed David's tendency to stop his shot

86

when he's trying to force it past mid-on. He was badly dropped several times by the Pakistanis at mid-on, leaning back rather than forward into the shot – not necessarily a fault, because it means you can hit the ball for six if you connect properly, but a fault when you fail to follow through with the shot.

Everyone in the game knows that you must pick up Geoff Boycott early on before he gets into his unhurried groove. Is he afraid of the really fast bowlers? All I can say is that Mike Hendrick always slips himself against Boycott and has definitely troubled him, while Alan Ward used to tickle him in the ribs early on, and Boycott didn't like it because he then hooked in the air a lot.

Mike Smith of Middlesex is one batsman Ian Buxton and I seemed to mesmerize whenever he played us. Because of his habit of falling over when playing the legside shot, I stumped him or Buxton bowled him every time for about five or six seasons, and Mike seemed powerless to alter that. It became a joke in the dressing room, and Mike Selvey had a good laugh after Buxton retired from the game. He found a newspaper cutting with the headline 'Buxton back for Derby'. It was about a junior foot-baller, but the Middlesex lads showed it to Mike Smith and pulled his leg unmercifully about the jinx placed on him by Ian Buxton.

There's always a plan for the class batsmen – with Dennis Amiss it's short-pitched fast bowling, with Derek Randall I'm looking for a stumping because he likes to use his feet against the spinners and tends to unbalance for legside shots. Clive Radley's a contender for the stumping as well, and if you contain him in his favourite mid-wicket area he'll get frustrated and take chances. Keith Fletcher's another who gets impatient if tied down. He doesn't give many chances in the bat/pad area because he plays well the fast one that comes into his ribs, but he'll play the short one outside the off stump with his bat away from his body. Keith's a very good player of spin bowling, so we'll normally bring the quickies back as soon as he comes in. Two great overseas bats-men, Clive Lloyd and Zaheer Abbas, have a weakness on the leg side. With Clive we'll have a man just behind square on the leg because he hits the full-length ball rather loosely and has a habit of chipping it in the air. And Zaheer plays the ball that's just short of a length on the leg stump in the air.

You know the weaknesses but also the strengths of the top batsman. You don't bowl on Dennis Amiss's leg stump because he's a superb on-driver, you don't give Mike Procter anything that's a full length, and Geoff Boycott and David Gower will murder anything short outside the off stump.

At Test level these tactical discussions are even more important. The night before the first day, the team will gather for dinner and eventually get round to discussing the opposition – and the keeper, because of his unique position in line with wicket and wicket, has a crucial tactical role to play. Those of us who'd toured Pakistan and New Zealand were in a good position to judge their qualities when they came over to England a few months later, and I think our professionalism and homework had a lot to do with our success.

Take the Pakistanis first. We knew that Haroon Rashid liked to play his shots, so we decided to get him playing outside the off stump and get him frustrated against typical English 'line and length' seam bowling. We worked on Haroon a little bit when touring Pakistan – after he'd hit us all over the place we'd say, 'Well played, but you won't be able to do that in English conditions.' He'd smile, but he did play loosely in England. I remember Chris Old bowling him through the gate at Lord's after he'd taken 14 in an over off Bob Willis – he was going for his shots in the last over before lunch.

We knew that Sadiq would struggle against short-pitched fast bowling interspersed with ones that leave the edge of the bat. He was afraid of the short ones and Bob Willis bowled very well against him – at Lord's he got him caught by me, fishing outside the off stump after having been tickled under the ribs. Mudassar was different – a brave player, technically sound, but he tended to hook in the air and we had him twice from poor hook shots in England. Javed Miandad and Wasim Raja were similar types – very fine stroke makers but impetuous and liable to fret if kept quiet for any length of time. With Bob Willis bowling fast and short to them, they never settled.

Our fast bowlers also had prearranged plans for the New Zealanders. Their best player, Geoff Howarth, was an experienced county batsman with Surrey, and although he made a lot of runs against us, he was never happy with the short one outside the off stump – a fact we always mentioned in our pre-Test discussions. John Wright, my Derbyshire colleague, also had an off-stump weakness. He'd altered his guard from leg stump to middle, and as a result was moving too far across and getting bowled too often. I told John about this when he played for Derbyshire, but when he turned out for New Zealand he was just another batsman to dismiss. I told our fast men, 'Just bowl it straight, he's been clean-bowled a lot on the New Zealand tour so far, he's leaving the gate open or getting too far across.' John never really did himself justice in the Test series as a result. Neither did Bev Congdon, a fine player with a good Test record. We worked out that Bev was a little long in the tooth now, and noticed his initial movement was always to get on the back foot. So the fast men would give him a couple on the breast bone then a really fast one on the off stump – and the slips and myself caught Bev a number of times. The same applied to Richard Hadlee, a brave fast bowler but not exactly lion-hearted with the bat. Every time we discussed Hadlee the batsman, Ian Botham would say, 'Just leave him to me, he's my rabbit.' And so it proved, with the obvious formula of two short-pitched ones aimed at the body and the next one getting him to fish with the bat away from the body.

It's been my privilege to play with some great cricket brains in the England side. Geoff Boycott is very good when we're fielding, and spots a batsman's weakness very swiftly; Mike Brearley's very wise indeed; and Bob Willis has exceptional mental clarity and memory for a fast bowler. But the best brain I've known was Ray Illingworth. He was terrific on that tour of Australia when he brought the Ashes back – whether it was hiding the poor fielders, handling the bowling changes astutely, making sure John Snow tried hard for the breakthrough, or generally getting the best out of his unfancied side. He really wanted to make you play for him.

When you talk about the wicketkeeper's responsibilities to the rest of the side, inevitably the question of his batting arises. I'm not saying that the keeper should be a batting passenger, but his responsibilities to the fielding side are so great that it's unfair to expect a major innings from him. Only Les Ames has really managed to be consistently brilliant at batting and keeping for a long period of time, but I feel the keeper's as much a specialist as a fast bowler – and whoever expected fifties from the quickie? The best keeper is worth the chance of losing 20 runs an innings when it's his turn to bat.

A classic case of too much being expected from the keeper came in the Lord's Test against New Zealand, when Bruce Edgar had to keep wicket. He'd been behind the stumps for over four hours on the Saturday, and yet when we were dismissed he was sent in as an opening bat! As an inexperienced lad, he must've been mentally shattered from standing for so many hours, and sure enough he played a tired shot early on to Bob Willis and was out cheaply. I thought it was unfair on a fine young prospect to give him so little time to unwind.

Because of batting considerations I could never really prove whether I was as good as Alan Knott at Test level. I've always felt my batting was underrated. I seem to do better abroad; I helped save two Tests in Pakistan by batting for a long time, and I partnered Ian Botham for a long spell when he was on his way to his maiden Test hundred in New Zealand. I prefer getting my head down. I'm not a natural stroke maker like Knotty, and when I have to go in with just ten overs left in a county match I don't look too special as I try to slog. So some people write me off as a batting novice. I only pushed Knotty for a Test place once – that was in the West Indies, when I got a good fifty against Jamaica, and with Knotty struggling both with the bat and behind the stumps I was told I was in with a chance for the next Test. But the selectors kept faith with Knotty – why shouldn't they? – and he came through his bad patch. I really admired him for the way he kept going for so long and for the bonus his batting gave to a mediocre batting line-up. Time after time he'd come in at 6 or 7 and turn the character of the game with his audacious stroke play.

Knotty and I have always been great friends. Before every Test match on tour, he'd come up to me and say, 'Bad luck, Bob.' I really appreciated that; as a professional sportsman, he knew how much I wanted to play rather than watch and he was always very understanding. A remark by Graham McKenzie neatly summed up how I'd feel on those occasions. 'You must really feel it at these social functions,' he said to me once in Australia. He was right – I was one of England's sixteen best cricketers on tour, I was effectively my country's second-best keeper, yet people would be coming up to me and saying, 'R. W. Taylor – who are you?'

Bill Lawry once told me that if he had to be reincarnated he'd like to return as the second wicketkeeper on a touring side because there were no pressures. I told him that was rubbish – a professional sportsman representing his country should always want to play for them. Knotty realized that – that's why we always got on so well. I think my presence helped keep him on his toes. One example of our great relationship: once at Sydney I was twelfth man against New South Wales. I felt drowsy, went outside the ground for a snooze under a shady tree, and forgot completely about my twelfth-man duties. Knotty was playing in the match, and when it was time for drinks he put on my blazer, sprinkled some talcum powder on his black hair to give him the familiar Taylor grey streak, and imitated my walk on the way to the wicket. It got a great laugh with players and spectators.

I think my disappointments in my early days with England helped me in the long run. There was the time in 1976 when Knotty was doubtful for the Test against the West Indies and the selectors didn't send for me but Roger Tolchard because they wanted batting stability. That's why Roger went on the India and Australia tour the following winter – and I told my wife, Cathy, to throw away my touring gear because I wouldn't need it any more. I was so disappointed because I'd have given anything to have attended the Melbourne Centenary Test, a unique occasion. Having never played against Australia in their continent at that time,

I wasn't eligible for the free trip laid on for the other English internationals. Another blow came in 1968 when, if you remember, England's tour to South Africa was called off because of the d'Oliveira affair. But the tour party was announced – and the number two to Alan Knott was John Murray, presumably because of his batting, because I'd played for the MCC against the Australians that year and by all reports had kept wicket well.

But I was never bitter. I was proud to be involved for my country – and when Mr Packer turned the cricket world upside down, I was ready. The moral for all you keepers at any level is this – remain philosophical, don't bear grudges on the field, keep fit, earn the respect of your team-mates, and that way you'll get as much happiness as I've had from a great game.

7 The Great Wicketkeepers

There's no such thing as a perfect wicketkeeper (the job's too difficult for a start), but these are my top keepers I've either played against or watched. I'd like to point out that all were in my opinion great keepers, and that their weaknesses are very much overshadowed by their assets.

KEITH ANDREW

Strengths
Quite simply, my idol. After all my years watching and playing first-class cricket, I've still seen nobody to touch him. Unflappable, neat, cool, his overall air of quiet competence was so impressive. Terrific technique, and he made it look so easy whether standing back to Frank Tyson at Northants or up to the difficult left-arm spinner George Tribe.

Weaknesses
No real technical faults, and I'm not speaking in nostalgic vein either. Perhaps a batting weakness – after all he only played in two Tests, because he couldn't be relied on to make runs in a crisis despite the vast amount of runs his brilliance would save behind the stumps. Taken for granted by many players, spectators and newsmen while playing for an unfashionable county, so there was never a danger of Keith being talked into the England team.

ABOVE *Keith Andrew*

WALLY GROUT

Strengths

A marvellous example in the field in a very enthusiastic side under Richie Benaud, a great judge of when to go for diving one-handed catches. Set a great standard of catching in that close ring of fielders like Benaud, Simpson and Davidson. Small and neat as Australian keepers go, he'd worked out a very good safety position on the crouch: his legs would be together instead of apart, his right foot flat and the left one behind the right heel with the left heel in the air. The hands would be above the knees in front of the face, and the overall effect was that the ball wouldn't often get past Wally Grout.

A genuinely nice man, I first met him in 1964 when he was twelfth man against Derbyshire. I listened open-mouthed as he

Wally Grout

gave me tips on motivation and technique and the importance of not moaning when you're not in the side. Wally, a great family man, gave me the idea of always having a family snapshot in my writing pad while touring. Four years later he was dead after a heart attack.

Weaknesses

Rather casual when taking straightforward catches. I can't forget the time when Ted Dexter snicked an easy one to Wally off Graham Corling in a Trent Bridge Test and Wally was throwing it up in triumph before the ball reached him. He dropped it. Perhaps he should have stood up to 'Slasher' Mackay in Tests because that would have made the batsmen play differently and perhaps brought some stumpings. After all Keith Andrew stood up to Ted Dexter, who was much more erratic than Mackay.

GODFREY EVANS

Strengths

Bouncy, extrovert, terrific in an overseas Test when it's over a hundred degrees and there's half an hour to go. A man for the big

Godfrey Evans

occasion, with a great Test-match temperament, he could also score quick runs against the clock. Must have been technically good to stand up the medium-paced Alec Bedser and to take Kent's difficult leg-break bowler Doug Wright for so many seasons.

Weaknesses

A bit too flashy with the dives when standing back. Perhaps he should have used his feet to get his body behind the ball, rather than opt for the spectacular dive that might impress some spectators but not the pros. Some of the old Derbyshire players have told me he didn't turn it on consistently for Kent in the way he did for England, so perhaps he lacked the mental strength to keep a certain standard going – the characteristic I admired so much in Keith Andrew.

96

JOHN WAITE

Strengths

Neat, unfussy, almost a taller version of Keith Andrew. Kept to some fine bowlers in Adcock, Heine, Tayfield and Peter Pollock, but he most impressed me one day in 1960 keeping to the South African skipper and opening bat Jackie McGlew. I was playing for the Minor Counties against the Springboks, and McGlew, a nondescript bowler, sent down five legside full tosses at me in one over. I missed them all, but I wasn't too humiliated to notice that John Waite took each one coolly and competently. His concentration was clearly first-class, because he was expecting to take the ball even when it should have been hammered to the boundary.

A fine, elegant batsman, in my opinion he was South Africa's greatest wicketkeeper.

John Waite

His batting must have sapped his energies at some stage. Although neat for one so tall (over six feet), he lacked agility in going for the wide chances on either side. Didn't keep to many slow bowlers in the Test side, apart from Tayfield, and he was clearly happier standing back. He wasn't speculative enough in going for those half-chances in front of the slips, perhaps because he'd worked out the angles, balanced the prospects against his height, and then trained himself to let them go to slip.

RODNEY MARSH

Strengths

Dedicated and tough, he really knuckled under to the disciplines needed to survive in Test cricket. Lost a lot of weight and toughened up both on and off the field after a difficult series against Ray Illingworth's side when his batting did much to keep him in the team. He's taken some of the greatest catches I've ever seen standing back – particularly one off Clive Lloyd down the leg

Rodney Marsh

side on the Rest of the World tour to Australia, when the left-hander swished at the right-hander bowling over the wicket and Marsh caught it full stretch with one hand. Made some astonishing retrievals in the series against Mike Denness's England side when Thomson and Lillee would sometimes slip erratic bouncing ones down the leg side. The problem was accentuated by the fact that the ball cuts swiftly through the thin air in Australia, and when it passes the bat it has a habit of dipping and swerving viciously – but Marsh coped superbly with the moving ball.

Weaknesses

Overreacts on and off the field when things don't go his way with either bat or ball. Gets over-emotional, can't seem to accept that you'll never master the game of cricket. Not too great standing up to the stumps – after all, in his time, the Aussies only had Mallett and O'Keefe bowling regular spin, and not turning it much either. Has the bad habit of turning his head away when the batsman plays the sweep off the slow bowler – doesn't keep his eye on the ball. Rather clumsy standing up, yet much more athletic and natural when standing back to the quicker bowlers. In that sense, very much a keeper of the modern era.

WASIM BARI

Strengths

At the top in Test cricket for a very long time – I know Alan Knott always rated him very highly, and so did I whenever Derbyshire played the Pakistanis. Neat and calm, a very versatile keeper who's stood up to some fine spinners – Intikhab, Mushtaq, Abdul Qadir, Javed Miandad, Iqbal Qasim, as well as pacemen like Asif Masood, Sarfraz Nawaz and Imran Khan. A brilliant judge of when to go for catches that mightn't reach first slip – one that stands out was at Headingley to get rid of Basil d'Oliveira. Very quick reactions and an ideal build.

99

Wasim Bari

The captaincy of his country preoccupied him so much that his decline was very sad to see. In the two series when he captained Pakistan against England he lost his enthusiasm and was guilty of the most elementary errors by his standards, like dropping returns, missing straightforward catches and failing to inspire the fielding side. Like myself and most other keepers I've known, he lacked the mental capacity to captain and keep wicket to the necessary standard.

ALAN KNOTT

Strengths

Probably England's best Test-match keeper. Magnificently consistent over a remarkable period of time, he was unfairly criticized on occasions just because he'd set such high standards, and so a human error would bring on the knockers. Agile, dedicated, he's my number two to Keith Andrew. Very good standing up, his close working relationship with Derek Underwood for Kent and England was mutually beneficial. Batting a bonus: he saved England many times with some daring innings. Terrific Test-match temperament.

Weaknesses

Perhaps over-dedicated. Almost a hypochondriac, he withdrew into himself on later tours, and as an experienced member of touring parties didn't do enough to lift morale when things were going wrong – especially on the 1974/5 tour to Australia. Didn't stand up enough to medium-pacers like Bob Woolmer or Tony Greig, and his batting must have distracted him sometimes from the main task of keeping wicket. Technically one fault – on occasions he didn't move his feet enough and went for one-handed takes to deliveries that weren't all that wide.

Alan Knott

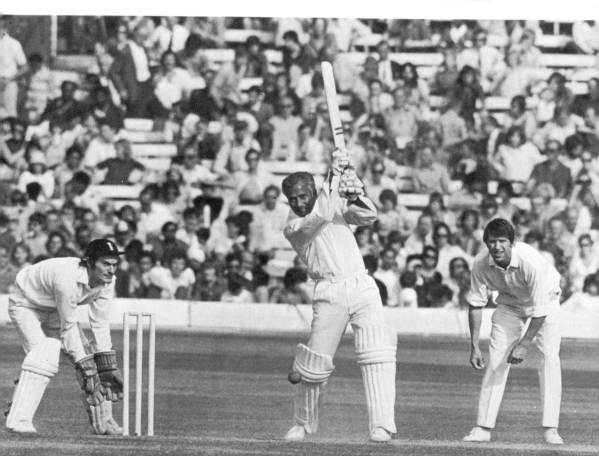

KEN WADSWORTH

Strengths

Easily New Zealand's best keeper, his death from cancer just two months after playing in the Prudential World Cup in England was a terrible blow. My opposite number in my first Test, his reactions were very quick. Nearly six feet tall, he triumphed over a physique that wasn't ideal for a keeper. I've seen him take some fine one-handed catches diving down the leg side off inside edges. Very good standing back to the quicks.

Weaknesses

Lacked mental toughness, and sometimes his work would get a little sloppy. Didn't play consistently at a high level – perhaps a few seasons in county cricket would have tightened up his technique. Didn't stand up to all that many slow bowlers, and he had Rodney Marsh's habit of averting his eyes when the batsman was going for the sweep or the ball pitched in the rough outside the leg stump.

Ken Wadsworth

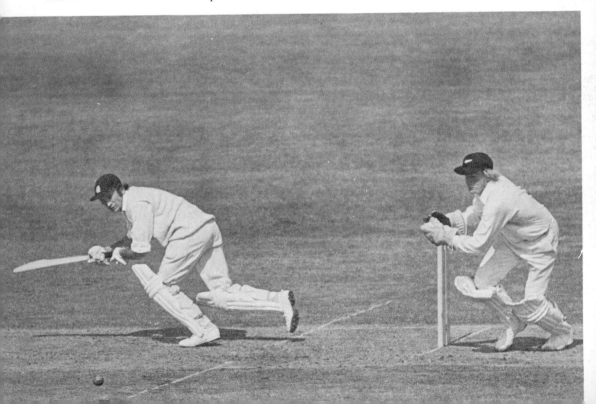

JIMMY BINKS

Strengths

Marvellously competent for so many years in county cricket. Kept to some great bowlers at Yorkshire and stood up to sharp bowlers like Tony Nicholson and Bob Appleyard. I've seen him make some marvellous legside stumpings off both. Physically strong, otherwise he wouldn't have kept wicket for 412 consecutive county matches. He must have needed strong character to keep going for so long, because he would have had many niggling injuries like chipped fingers and strains.

Weaknesses

Towards the end of his county career, he seemed to lapse in concentration. I was a little disappointed he let things slide – after all he was only thirty-three when he retired. Perhaps the problems at Yorkshire got to him eventually. He should have challenged Evans, Parks and Murray harder for the England spot. But in the end he seemed to prefer playing for Yorkshire to touring with England.

8 The Great Batsmen

A wicketkeeper's in a great position to judge a batsman – his speed of footwork, his placement of shots, his ability to concentrate, and his weaknesses. I've had the great pleasure of playing with or against all these batsmen, and each, in his own distinct way, deserves the adjective 'great'.

ROHAN KANHAI

Strengths

The number one in my book, a complete player on all types of wickets. Learned his trade on the bouncy West Indian wickets, but his spell in the Lancashire League toughened up his technique. He mellowed from being an erratic but brilliant batsman to a master. Two shots he played against Derbyshire I'll never forget – a six over mid-wicket off the front foot to a good-length fast ball from Alan Ward that pitched outside the off stump, and an even more remarkable six off Mike Hendrick. It was a straight low full toss, going at knee height. A normal bloke would have played the ball down, but Rohan got under it and hit it for a mid-wicket six.

There was a great bad-wicket hundred against us at Coventry. On a turning, lifting, bouncing track, he made 187 not out in an all-out total of 295. Unlike Gary Sobers, he was cool at the crease and had great mental powers.

Weaknesses

A tendency to play risky shots early in his innings. A bad knee injury didn't help towards the end of his days at Warwickshire. Went out of Test cricket too early: the strains of captaincy told. He was never much of a team man, and as I found out when touring with him in the Rest of the World side, he was a bit of a loner.

Rohan Kanhai

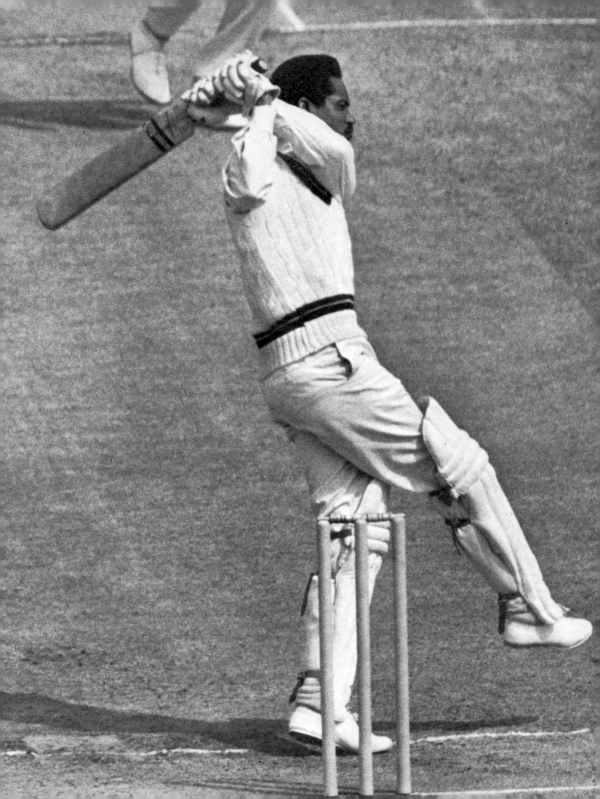

GARY SOBERS

Strengths

Surely the greatest all-rounder in cricket history, he was a marvellously fluent batsman with literally every shot. Consistent
genius – a great attacking batsman at Test level for a remarkable
number of years. He played the best innings I've ever seen on the
Rest of the World tour when he made 254 against an Australian
eleven. He was on a 'king pair' (Dennis Lillee had got him) and he
had domestic worries on his mind, yet he played the most perfect
knock. He never gave a chance, and the Aussies just couldn't bowl
at him.

A really big hitter, some of his sixes in that famous 36-run over
off Malcolm Nash were mishits, yet they still went for 6. One shot
over long off against Derbyshire sticks in my memory – the
off-spinner Edwin Smith bowled Gary one that pitched in the
rough outside his off stick; Gary kept his head down, and as it
pitched in the rough he hit it straight over long off. It was a golf
shot, but what a demoralizing one to play!

Weaknesses

Would give you a chance early on outside the off stump, and woe
betide you if you didn't snap it up. Didn't do himself justice with
Nottinghamshire, probably because he was playing in a mediocre
side and he was hailed as the miracle worker, but also because his
mental attitude wasn't good enough. He became preoccupied
with golf and racing, and it was common knowledge on the county
circuit that Gary would only bat for a certain length of time if he
wanted to watch a race on the television. I'd say things like, 'What
have you backed today, Gary?' and he'd tell you and lose his
concentration. The strain of captaining his adopted county eventually told, and bowling distractions didn't help either.

VIV RICHARDS

Strengths

A cold-eyed killer with the bat, who can humiliate good bowlers by banging them past mid-wicket when they think they've done him outside the off stump. Great hitter of the ball on the 'up', the shot through mid-wicket off his toes is a beauty. Great all-round-the-wicket player, although his real forte is the leg side. Fine big-match temperament.

Weaknesses

Because he goes for the shots all the time you can trap him early on, especially on or outside the off stump. Gets too confident, makes too many brilliant seventies when they should be really big scores. Likes to go down the wicket, so there's always a stumping chance. As he gets older his eye and reactions will dim, and time will tell if he'll become a Kanhai and tighten up his technique.

Viv Richards

BARRY RICHARDS

Strengths

A great all-round technique meant he could destroy any bowling side when he really felt like it. On his day, a hundred before lunch is a formality and you just can't bowl at him. All the shots – you don't score 325 not out in a day in a Sheffield Shield match unless you can attack. Played the hook shot down onto the ground very well. Poised and calm, a fine bad-wicket player. Hampshire

Barry Richards

should have sponsored him for scoring a certain amount of runs in a season; if they had, Barry would have broken many batting records. He and Gordon Greenidge made a great opening pair with their contrasting styles. Didn't have a chance to prove himself consistently in Tests, but I'm sure that the challenge would have made him an even better player.

Weaknesses

Didn't relish the occasional fast short-pitched delivery. Lacked concentration, had to motivate himself and often failed – once while playing for T. N. Pearce's eleven towards the end of the season I saw him get out deliberately on the Saturday night so he wouldn't have to be at the ground on time for the resumption of his innings on Monday morning.

Unlike Greenidge, he wasn't a great team man. Too money-conscious; he talked too much about earning a lot of cash and gave the false impression to the public that cricketers were always on the make. Unless he thought he was getting well paid, he wouldn't exactly hammer himself into the ground for his side.

GRAEME POLLOCK

Strengths

One of the hardest hitters I've known in the game, great eye and marvellous timing. Astonishingly mature for such a youngster when he first entered Test cricket. Authoritative way of batting – with his long reach he could annihilate Test attacks. Unlike Barry Richards he'd had a consistent spell of high scoring in Tests: when South Africa were banned from international cricket, his batting average was 60. Eddie Barlow told me that Graeme made him look a complete novice when they had their huge partnership against Australia in 1964 at Adelaide. They put on 341, Eddie made a double hundred and Graeme 175 (at the age of nineteen!), yet Eddie said he was completely overshadowed by the left-hander.

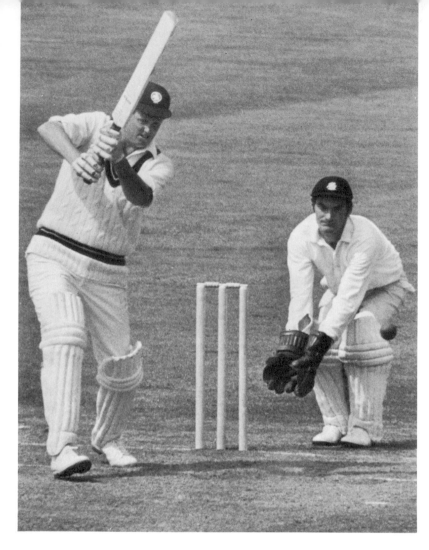

Graeme Pollock

Weaknesses

Not a tight defence, and the fact that he didn't always get his right foot across meant he was occasionally vulnerable outside the off stump. Hit the ball with the bat a long way from the body, so he wouldn't be the best bet to survive on a spiteful wicket. On the Rest of the World tour to England in 1970 he was clean-bowled six times in eight innings against England, so he wasn't a totally compact player.

TOM GRAVENEY

Strengths

A classic, mature middle-order English batsman. Consistent, elegant, with his long reach he played the spinners particularly well. With a straight pick-up he played in the 'V' like all the classic batsmen – the 'V' being the area between mid-off and mid-on, on either side of the wicket.

Found gaps in the field with immense ease – his timing was superb. A lovely offside player, he always seemed to know where his off stump was and could pick the line up very swiftly. Played some great knocks on rain-affected wickets over the years in Derbyshire. Nearly forty-three when he finished second in the national averages with 62, he was 'Mr Consistency' for many years.

Weaknesses

Sometimes allowed you to bowl at him. Almost as passive as Colin Cowdrey when he was out of sorts, he could be over-elegant and pinned down too easily on the leg stump. Once in a Gillette Cup match against us he won the 'Man of the Match' award for his batting even though Worcestershire lost the match because Tom didn't get his runs quickly enough.

Tom Graveney

Didn't do himself justice in the England side till he was forty – partly because the selectors didn't trust him and partly because Tom didn't care about their opinions. The fact that he turned himself out of the England side because he wanted to play in a benefit match for himself during a Test proved his indifference to their wishes. Despite his great record, his figures could have been even more impressive.

COLIN COWDREY

Strengths

Impeccable technique, well coached, a model for all youngsters. A great theorist and enthusiast, he loved to practise in the nets, and I've spent many happy hours with him on Australian tours. On his best days his timing was so perfect that the fielder would always lose the chase for the ball whether it was on a small or a large ground. Like Graveney, he got into line perfectly and his pick-up was straight.

On the 1974/5 tour to Australia, Colin was the unanimous choice to come out to help our injury-hit team. Although he didn't make many big scores he was very brave and got behind the line all the time against Lillee and Thomson. It was quite a performance at the age of forty-two. Played the off drive beautifully but could also do the unorthodox – his paddle shot (following the ball round from the off-spinner and playing it fine) gave me the shock of my life when I first saw it because the ball went like a rocket past my feet.

Weaknesses

Introspective and over-theoretical. It seems funny to admit it, but he lacked confidence in his great batting gifts. Could be kept quiet by bowlers he really should have slaughtered. Unlike other great batsmen, your heart wasn't in your mouth if bowling at Colin. Almost too stylish, didn't let himself go enough. Should have been an even more superb batsman in terms of figures.

GEOFF BOYCOTT

Strengths

A self-made player who by dint of massive determination has manufactured himself into a great opening batsman. He's an amazing concentrator with a good defence – I saw him score a fine unbeaten hundred against Pakistan in Hyderabad when he had to bat all day on a rough wicket where the ball was keeping low. Defensively a master batsman, technically one of the best I've seen on a bad wicket. Five-day Test cricket is tailor-made for him. He'll save you many games, although if his side bats first he could win it by getting a big score. Lovely player off the back foot outside the off stick. When he goes to the crease I have every confidence that he'll get a hundred for England.

Weaknesses

Limited strokes, doesn't dictate to the bowlers, although on occasions he's proved he can hit hard. His batting partner always has to score quickly to compensate for Boycott's obsession with staying at the crease. The worst hour's batting I've ever had was in a

Test in New Zealand when he was captain. I went in as night- OPPOSITE *Ian Chappell*
watchman, and he didn't give me a word of advice apart from
saying, 'Watch the singles' – ironic really, because his running
between the wickets is shocking for a batsman of his class and
experience. Everyone in the game knows about this, and his
batting partner must always watch his step.

The captaincy of Yorkshire and England complicated the personality of an already complicated, proud man. It was a boyhood
ambition to skipper first his county, then his country, yet he
couldn't see that the best skippers aren't always the best players.
The pressure really got to him in New Zealand, and his batting
suffered due to his being captain.

A mixed-up, complex man, but England are always a more
difficult side to beat when Boycott's in the team.

IAN CHAPPELL

Strengths

A better player than he looked, he had to work at his game. Very
good on the leg side, his superb eye meant he could get away with
working the ball to leg from the off stump. God's gift to a Test side
– a captain worth his place in the team on sheer ability. Great
concentration and a good player of spin, he was a real winner. The
captaincy didn't affect his batting; he seemed to thrive on it.

Weaknesses

A tendency to get chest-on with his legs too close together meant
he was vulnerable to lbw's against high pace. Bouncers from John
Snow and South Africa's Mike Procter and Peter Pollock made
him a sucker for the hook shot, which he kept playing in the air.

Headstrong and undiplomatic, I've been in his company at
cocktail parties and been embarrassed by his language to selectors. Had a lot to do with the decline in behaviour in the
Australian side of the mid-Seventies.

117

GREG CHAPPELL

Strengths

More elegant than Ian, although almost as fond of the leg side. Toughened up his technique when playing early on for Somerset, had a nice stance and plenty of time to play the ball. Ian's first movement was always back, but Greg would stand still and go forward if the ball was well pitched up. A classical-looking batsman.

Weaknesses

A bad starter who also hooked in the air. Bob Willis rattled him with the short stuff. Although Greg was a much better looking batsman, I think Ian was more effective. The captaincy of his country didn't suit Greg as a batsman, although it helped mature him as a man. Seemed to get distracted while batting for his young, inexperienced Australian team when they were badly beaten 3–0 by Mike Brearley's England. Got dispirited, and it showed in his batting, because the concentration had gone.

ZAHEER ABBAS

Strengths

Lovely offside player and good timer of the ball. A big innings man, his first Test knock in England was a magnificent 274 at the age of twenty-three. Despite his longing for crease-occupying, he could never be boring.

Very good through mid-wicket, he plays the spinners and medium-pacers best. One of the most consistent Test and county players of the Seventies.

Tends to play away from his body and doesn't get his left foot far enough over. Can be troubled by anyone genuinely quick, and has a habit of hooking in the air. His pick-up is rather flowery, and he brings the bat in from third man, so he must be a candidate for a good fast yorker. Yet his magnificent eye seems to get him out of trouble many times.

Zaheer Abbas